THE
END
OF
DEATH

THE
END
of
DEATH
Making Peace With God

By Richard C. MacLeay

XULON PRESS

Xulon Press
555 Winderley Pl, Suite 225
Maitland, FL 32751
407.339.4217
www.xulonpress.com

Paperback ISBN-13: 978-1-66289-047-5
Ebook ISBN-13: 978-1-66289-048-2

Contents

INTRODUCTION

Overview of the Book

B eginning with a quick overview of the subject at hand the reader can stay focused on the scope of study undertaken in this book. I suggest that you do not stop reading at this overview but read the full text of the book to understand how the subjects are based on ancient Scripture, the Bible.

This book is a thematic study of the subject of death as the punishment for sin. Sin is any disobedience or rebellion to God's perfect holiness and order in the creation He has made. It is difficult for any person in today's world to understand that death was a result of a self-willed independence from God, but the Bible reveals that this was the case. Death is so "natural" it is hard to see that it was optional in the beginning. God clearly warned Adam of the penalty of death for disobedience. Is a reversal possible whereby all death can be removed from God's kingdom? The plan of God revealed in the Bible is that God is working to bring the end of death.

In the beginning God created the world as a testing ground for humanity where the men and women He made in God's image could grow and prosper in their personal choices of life and good. Adam and Eve failed. God could have destroyed them immediately, but their sin brought a sentencing to death from a righteous God. That took place as a legal process, not a summary judgment.

The sentence of death was not an immediate execution of Adam and Eve, but the sentence was sure. The whole creation came under that condemnation. The process of death in the world began when God spoke to Adam and Eve after they sinned but was slow enough to allow God to provide a deliverance from eternal death before the final judgment. The penalty of physical death became universal, but the penalty of eternal punishment (the second death) was not enforced until the final judgment of the world.

The mixture of life and death in the creation is the big mystery in the experience of life. God shared the wonder of His life with the created physical world, but men and women failed to live righteously to the glory of God.

———————+———————

The mixture of life and death in the creation is the big mystery in the experience of life.

The present world is a mixture of God-given life and the progressive death of that life. This is why the average person loves life and hates it at the same time. It is also a mixture of spiritual life and spiritual death because we are made in the image of God who is Spirit. Death is a physical and spiritual reality and is the source of all the pain in our lives.

The Bible teaches that the entrance of death was a righteous punishment for the rebellion made long ago against God. God pronounced death as a punishment for disobedience. This is also called the curse of death. People might not think Adam and Eve are relevant to the modern world but then the reality of death surrounds them and they find themselves conforming to death, sometimes consciously and sometimes unconsciously. Although the death process is progressing as the destruction of life physically and spiritually, God has a plan to end the curse of death and restore all persons to God's original purpose of eternal life with Himself, if they are willing. This is called God's plan of salvation.

Mankind is under the curse of death now. Every person has chosen their own way of life and is alienated from God, imitating the choices of Adam and Eve. Like the cruise ship Titanic after its hull was ruptured, mankind is under the curse of death and cannot help but sink. God allows a lifetime to get into his lifeboat, but after that there is no opportunity to escape the final judgment of eternal death. In the Bible this final judgment is called "the second death." God's love provides a lifeline of forgiveness and a new life to replace the death-walk of the curse of death.

The world will sink under the curse of death, but God has a kingdom coming that will be filled with all persons who accept the forgiveness of sin and reconciliation with God provided freely in Jesus Christ. God is accomplishing this saving mission of mercy by His plan of salvation and the end of death will be individually experienced by those persons who believe in Jesus.

SOME LITERARY CONVENTIONS EXPLAINED

If I capitalize the word "Man," the meaning is homo-sapiens, or mankind, according to traditional sense. Sometimes I use "human" or "humanity" with the same meaning as "Man" or "mankind" because people nowadays are sensitive to gender.

I use pronouns in their traditional meanings. Often people choose to capitalize pronouns referring to Deity, as a style. Style should not be confused with doctrine. I use capitalization of direct references to God in heaven. What then do we do with Jesus? I will follow modern Bible translations not using capitalization of pronouns. Greek was simpler because they just wrote in all capital letters!

As a practice I capitalize pronouns referring to God or the Father in heaven, and not to those referring to Jesus. This allows some clarity when referring to Jesus and his Father in the same sentence. The use of "he" should not be thought as doctrinally exclusive of Deity. Jesus is fully "He" and fully "he," and the use of the one does not deny the other. Among the twenty-one versions of the Bible I researched for this study, only one capitalized the pronouns referring to Jesus.

I use the editing style of Bible translations such as the English Standard Version and many others as I blend the Scriptures into my writing. I follow the biblical translation style that does not capitalize many words that some authors choose to capitalize in their literary works. Because I quote the Scriptures so often, I follow the style of the Bible translators. In this way the flow of the commentary and the Scriptures is maintained.

This book is a study of what God has made, and specifically of the life He has given us to live on the earth. The perspective is thoroughly biblical. I believe the Bible is the divinely inspired written revelation of divine purposes and intentions. There is no book like it in age, breadth, and scope of the human soul. It has proven itself as the treasure house of spiritual guidance for hundreds of generations. It is our primary source about who God is and what He is like. It is the measure by which all personal revelation is judged. The more we study it with sincere hearts, with commonsense interpretations, and with the guidance of the living Spirit of God, the better we will order our lives in God's will.

Therefore, I have chosen to reference the Scriptures often, so that the reader may evaluate personally the doctrines explained in this study. Direct quotations of verses are integrated into the text in bold typeface, with translation referenced, with the purpose of letting the Spirit of God educate the reader directly from the Word of God. KJV=King James (Authorized Version). MKJV=Modern King James Version. ESV=English Standard version. TLV=Tree of Life Version. CEV=Contemporary English Version. I cite the references with the full book names to help young Bible scholars look up references more quickly. Specific versions are quoted that best express the original languages and culture but with contemporary word clarity.

Quotations are often integrated into the text because I am not presenting a theory and then "proof-texting" it. I am bringing together the Scriptures to reveal the truths in them. This is what Jesus did. **"Was it not necessary that the Christ should suffer these things and enter into his glory?" And beginning with Moses and all the Prophets, he interpreted to them in all the Scriptures the things concerning himself** (Luke 24:26-27 ESV).

I acknowledge my debt to all faithful believers who before me have written, preached, taught, discussed, and sometimes debated with me, and whose countless influences have been a blessing. Any errors are my own, and hopefully they are few.

Part 1

The Entrance of Death

O LORD, you are my God; I will exalt you; I will praise your name, for you have done wonderful things, plans formed of old, faithful and sure. Isaiah 25:1 ESV

Genesis is the Book of Beginnings

God has given us the first book in the Bible named Genesis which means "Beginnings." At the beginning of this study on the end of death many characters and subjects in the first pages of Genesis will be introduced. I apologize for the difficulty of keeping all the unfamiliar terms and ideas in your head at the same time. This is not unlike your family moving to a new city when you are required to jump right into a new school where everyone has known each other for years. It is a bit overwhelming to meet twenty-five or more new people in a day. Genesis can be like that.

In the first part of this book, I will introduce ideas and themes that will be repeated and explained further as we go along in the study. Do not let them confuse you. As we get into the subject of the end of death, you will begin to understand the terms and relationships of the new ideas, so that they will not seem as unconnected as at the beginning.

Also, when we study Adam and Eve as the first man and the first woman, the differences of male and female do not make much difference in the outcome of this study. The curse of death was given because of personal sin, falling the same on them both. God had the same requirement of making good choices for both. Male or female, all of us are humankind first, and death affects us equally. God's judgment is on sin and is not based on gender. Gender is real and created by God, but the first chapters of Genesis are focused on the beginning of sin in the world that brought death to men and women alike.

If you have not recently read Genesis chapters 1-3, then you should do so now before reading further. Having the creation account fresh in your thinking will help with comprehension of the text.

In common biblical usage, the proper name "Adam" is often also translated "man" and came from a generic term for the human God made. Therefore, the Bible teaches that generic "Man" was created by God as male and female (Genesis 1:27).

When Adam first saw Eve, he did not see her as his competition but as his completion. He was rejoicing in their likeness to one another. Eve was created to fulfill Adam's need for another living soul *like himself*. No animal was able to meet that need (Genesis 2:20). I guess for Adam it was love at first sight after reviewing all the animals and finding not one like himself.

God issues his forgiveness, healing, revelation, redemption, rewards, and honor to anyone regardless of gender. In the New Testament, the apostle Paul wrote, **There is neither Jew nor Greek, there is neither slave nor free, there is no male and female, for you are all one in Christ Jesus** (Galatians 3:28 ESV).

Therefore, the presence of sin is not gender related. Sin is the big problem for men and women alike. Genesis, as the book of beginnings, recorded the specific sin of Adam that brought the judgment of death into the whole world.

THE DEPTH OF SIN

Genesis is a book of beginnings. Following the creation of Adam and Eve, another first event in the garden of God was their sin. We usually refer to this as "Adam's sin" following the discussions of the apostle Paul in his letter to the church in Rome. The entrance of sin by the first couple had disastrous results. From the beginning the tempter, who is also called "the serpent," brought out the big lie. "You will not die if you disobey God," he told Eve. How wrong that was!

When God personally warned Adam that death was the result of disobedience, He was serious (Genesis 2:16,17). The first Adam led us into ruin through his disobedience by eating the fruit God had forbidden (not that any of us would have done differently). The main principle illustrated by eating the fruit was disobedience to God (Genesis 3:17). It was self-will and a lack of faith in what God had said. The history of the world has proven how great an act of sin that was.

Most importantly, by Adam's sin God's original plan to make us stewards over His world was derailed. God presented Adam with his plan in Genesis 1.

> **So God created man in his own image, in the image of God he created him; male and female he created them. And God blessed them. And God said to them, "Be fruitful and multiply and fill the earth and subdue it, and have dominion over the fish of the sea and over the birds of the heavens and over every living thing that moves on the earth."** Genesis 1:27-28 (ESV).

God created humanity to naturally mature without the hardship of sin that resulted in death. Before sin, **The LORD God took the man and put him in the garden of Eden to work it and keep it** (Genesis 2:15 ESV). After sin, because of the curse on sinful behavior, God decreed to put Man (the male and the female) out of the garden in Eden to bear the consequences of their sins in toilsome work and pain, until they died and returned to dust (Genesis 3:23-24).

God in His mercy made us in the beginning to know Him who is the source of goodness, life, and glory.

God in His mercy made us in the beginning to know Him who is the source of goodness, life, and glory. This was a wondrous initiation into life, and all glory for it goes to God. After Man's sin earned the punishment of death, the history of the world has become a long painful struggle with death. In love God was determined to bring us back to Himself.

DEATH FOLLOWS SIN

The subject of death can be quite broad. There is a literal meaning of "death" as well as figurative ones. There are usages that appear spiritual, and those that are physical. I want to narrow the subject in this study to some of the theological (the study of God) and soteriological (the study of salvation) aspects of death. We are not trying to force an interpretation on the word "death," but we want to understand the meaning of how the word is being used in Scripture.

Sometimes an academic style seems impersonal, so this book is not written to be rigorously academic. However, there is a need for every Christian to grow in knowledge. Study should not be merely academic, but revelatory of the wonderful grace and love of God toward us in Jesus Christ. Understanding and believing the gospel of Jesus is a life and death matter. With God, it is always personal. I know sometimes I wander from the third person to the second person, from "they" to "you." It is because God cannot love the world without loving YOU!

_____+_____

Understanding and believing the gospel of Jesus is a life and death matter. With God, it is always personal.

_____

It might seem that Man is the center of the universe when we study the subject of death. God and His glory ought to be the center. Man became the center of attention because sin entered through Adam, and death followed sin as a judgment upon sinners (the curse), turning the world upside down. Paul plainly said, **Wherefore, as by one man sin entered into the world, and death by sin; and so death passed upon all men, for that all have sinned** (Romans 5:12 KJV). A sinful attitude ignores God

_____+_____

God cannot love the world without loving YOU!

_____

and gives humanity top billing. The gospel of Jesus puts God back on top.

If your Bible knowledge is limited, you may not be familiar with the biblical idea of lineage. Lineage is life passing from one generation to the next. At the beginning, God created life with the ability to reproduce "after its kind" (Genesis 1:21, 24, 25, 28, 29). Modern science agrees that life can only come from life but does not know where the first life came from. The Bible acknowledges that life began with God. Every generation bears the genetic markings of its forebears, for good or bad. After Adam's sin the life he and Eve passed on to their children was tainted with death.

Adam was legally, genetically, and spiritually responsible for all future generations when he passed physical life on to his children. Therefore, his sin was called "the fall of Man" into sin and death. The curse of death has passed to all following generations. There is a spiritual aspect to this death also. Death is a curse that Adam brought on himself and us, and it was contrary to the desire of God who wanted to share all the good things of His life with the people He had made.

BEYOND PHYSICAL DEATH

We experience life as flesh *and* spirit. Science can declare life is only a physical process, but our own consciousness knows this is naïve. Science discovers fascinating truths about physical things but does not satisfy the soul. Life is bigger than science because "science" is being continually updated as a consensus of the inventory of knowledge.

The pursuit of a career in science is based on faith that there are unknowns yet to be discovered in an ordered universe. Our spiritual nature is God-given. God describes himself as existence and creator by his name, **I Am Who I Am** (Exodus 3:14 ESV). All true science admits there are unknowns. Certainly, there are yet many unknowns in knowledge of God.

Human consciousness perceives the existence of a spiritual dimension as well as a physical one.

Humanity's problem is deeper than death, although most people do not see it that way. Humanity's problem is the origin of physical death; Man's struggle is with the righteous God who pronounced death on sinful behavior. The deeper biblical revelation answers the question: Where did death come from? The cure for death will not arise from human science. The cure for death is found in the forgiveness of God and His gift of everlasting life. He will counter all the effects of death by correcting the sin that brought death in the first place.

He will counter all the effects of death by correcting the sin that brought death in the first place.

God in the Bible described death in two parts, physical death and "the second death" (Revelation 20:6). Humanity is subject to physical *and* spiritual existence. **It is appointed unto men once to die, but after this the judgment** (Hebrews 9:27 KJV). The Bible reveals to us that life continues past physical death. Many people think death is simply the end of consciousness. Many other people think persons who are dead become free-ranging angels in a spiritual dimension. The Bible does not support either idea.

Physical death alone does not solve the sin problem because God is not satisfied by punishing sin. He wants to restore humanity to righteousness. Punishment of sin satisfies divine justice, but God is also loving toward his creation. That is why He gave the revelation of the destruction of this world at the end of this age and prophesied its replacement with righteousness.

Since all these things are thus to be dissolved, what sort of people ought you to be in lives of holiness and godliness, waiting for and hastening the coming of the day of God, because

7

of which the heavens will be set on fire and
dissolved, and the heavenly bodies will melt
as they burn! But according to his promise we
are waiting for new heavens and a new earth in
which righteousness dwells.

(2 Peter 3:11-13 ESV).

THE "VERY GOOD" CREATION
WAS NOT PERFECT

God's original intent for humanity is found in the text of
Genesis. A few short chapters will not give us all the detail we
might like, but God has given us enough for a fuller revelation
of God's "big picture."

At the end of the first chapter of Genesis, God surveyed the
wonderous works He had made, and He pronounced it "very
good." On hearing this most preachers announce that everything was "Perfect!"

Personally, I do not equate the pronouncement of "very
good" with "perfect." Perhaps the greatest difficulty in evangelism is trying to deal with the average person's frustration
with the prevalence and persistence of evil in the world. If you
mention the love of God, they respond that a loving God would
not make such a messed-up world. The "very good" world in
Genesis was still subject to a fall into sin, decay, and death. We
should acknowledge that fact. But neither was sin God's fault.

I am not aiming for "very good" on my morals scorecard
because Jesus did not set "very good" as our goal. I think that
Jesus chose his words purposefully in the sermon on the mount.
**You therefore must be perfect, as your heavenly Father is per-
fect** (Matthew 5:48 ESV). Jesus meant to use the wording "be
perfect" to push us beyond "very good" because he said God
is perfect. I am looking for perfection, as Jesus taught.

You might think that now I have dug a theological hole
for myself! Did God make something that was not perfect?

God did not make a mistake. The creation of the universe was exactly according to plan. It was "very good."

A mother is not disparaged for giving birth to a baby who does not know its hand from a teething ring. Maturity is another category beyond birth. As it turned out, the man and woman whom God created, and the beautiful planet He created to be inhabited, were not immune to a worrisome mixture of beauty and beast. This is not to caste dispersion on immaturity as if it were sin. But neither is it perfection. God places value on maturity (John 7:17, Hebrews 5:13,14). God created the world "very good" and sinless; but sin was possible. God expected mankind to mature without sinning. When Adam and Eve sinned, everything changed.

There is no mention of death in the creation until Genesis 2:17. The first mention comes in a warning to the man, Adam, not to eat of the tree of the knowledge of good and evil. The outcome, God said, will be his death.

I do not know the extent of the vocabulary of Adam at this point in his life. He had not yet begun naming all the animals. There was no mention of anything dying yet. That is why the world that God had made was called "very good." Adam did not have a lot of experience, but Adam was created wise enough to know "to die is bad, to live is good." Adam was young and inexperienced, but God still expected him to obey a commandment personally spoken to him.

This was the state of the "very good" world in Genesis at the beginning: Creation was wonderful, but death was still possible, or God would not have warned against it. All was not "perfect" (i.e., mature) because everything was new-born (Genesis 3:1). God had a word for death although nothing had died; and Adam was warned about death.

And the LORD God commanded the man, saying, "You may surely eat of every tree of the garden, but of the tree of the knowledge

**of good and evil you shall not eat, for in the
day that you eat of it you shall surely die"**
Genesis 2:16-17 ESV.

Was there sin already elsewhere in the universe? God had
created spiritual beings like angels also, but the creation narrative focused on our physical universe instead. Somewhere
in this timeframe the devil rebelled. Genesis referred only to
the types of life God had created in the earth.

It seems likely that there was rebellion in the angelic ranks
by the time God warned Adam about the consequence of disobedience. The creation of mankind on the earth became
new ground for the devil to corrupt with his rebellion. Would
humanity side with God or the devil? The subject of death was
relevant to Adam because of God's warning, in any case.

God gave Adam authority in the earth. He did not realize at
this point that his fall into sin could affect all creatures under
his dominion, and even the earth itself (Genesis 3:17, **cursed
is the ground because of you**). It is true that all of us sin with
little understanding of the implications and ripple effects of
our deeds. An off-the-cuff insult in our thoughts can be our
own "irresistible fruit" so that we think only of the momen-
tary pleasure of speaking it out loud rather than considering
the long-term damage it works in the heart and spirit. Have
you considered where God has given you authority in your
sphere of influence? Beware of the ripple effects of your mis-
used authority.

The description "very good" was perfectly appropriate
to the world God created in Genesis 1. Yes, death was possible, but not initiated. Death should have been avoided. God
had a wonderful purpose in mind when He created Man with
the ability and responsibility to choose right or wrong. When
death came in, the world turned deadly. Death was not God's
fault if God gave warning of the consequences of sin to Adam,
along with the ability to resist it. This is what Genesis tells us
about death in the beginning.

THE POSSIBILITY OF TEMPTATION

The book of Genesis reveals that the world was brought into existence by a personal God and not merely a chance physical process (Genesis 1:1-3). Its form and fashion gave glory to the master designer, engineer, and creator of all physical elements. Adam was God's unique mix of body and spirit. Let history begin! Indeed, the world was "very good" in the very best way because there was no sin in it.

Man was created in the image of God. But even with all the magnificence of his design, he was not yet tested. God wanted it so at the beginning.

Man was created by design. The magnificence of the design was revealed when God said his human being had been made "in the image of God." Godlikeness was built into both the man and the woman (see Matthew 23:37 where God compares himself to a mother hen with her chicks). Godlikeness was a high honor and a high calling. God was smarter than to waste His time designing a capacity for Godlikeness within us, only to leave us on a natural animal level.

I suppose someone could argue that God was to blame for creating a world with the possibility of evil. We do not yet understand many things. In eternity He will show us the greater wisdom of giving us the ability to choose life, rather than evil. It was not our choice to make ourselves as we are, so we must face the fact that we were created to discern and implement right or wrong choices by divine design. Maturity is our divine calling.

THE GARDEN OF EDEN

The world at the beginning featured a garden in Eden where Man (male and female) was tested by the commandment to not eat of the fruit of the tree of knowledge. Also, the tree of life was there (Genesis 2:9). Man was not created "perfect" but sinless. He was able to fall. The command not to eat from one tree was a test.

Eden was a "very good" place, but it was designed to be transitional for humanity. The presence of the two special trees shows that Eden was not an end. When they disobeyed, their violation of the tree of knowledge led to expulsion from the garden. If they had obeyed, Adam and Eve would have required fruit from the tree of life to move into eternity (Genesis 3:22). Either way, Adam's and Eve's days in Eden were numbered. It is doubtful they lived there long. Without sin they could have stayed longer and continued to grow in fellowship with God. With sin, they were locked outside the garden gates.

In the Genesis narrative, those two trees required significant mention in Genesis 2:9. Interestingly, access was not forbidden to the tree of life, but only the tree of knowledge (Genesis 2:16,17). Apparently, Adam and Eve did not eat the fruit from the tree of life before they sinned. After they sinned, access was blocked (Genesis 3:22,23). Sinners and eternal life do not mix. I think that the presence of the tree of life in the garden was an indication of God's intention and hope that Adam and Eve would not sin but remain in the garden to mature. Sadly, that did not happen.

The entrance of sin caused a change of venue for mankind's development. The curse on them extended to all creation, and the first man and first woman were ejected from environmental abundance in the garden to the relative poverty of a world cursed because of their own disobedience.

What was God's plan for a transition from the garden in Eden to eternal life if Adam had not sinned? We are not told. We have the accounts of the bodily carrying away of Enoch and Elijah into heaven for comparative speculation. They are unusual for being translated into heaven while alive. Paul said there will be an instant change in those remaining alive when Jesus returns (1 Corinthians 15:51). These are clues as to what might have been the model of transition for humans from earth to eternity if there had been no sin.

Sin Separates from God

Adam and Eve both sinned concerning the first tree by disobeying God and eating from it. The curse was a pronouncement of death on them for disobedience. This sin broke the intimate relationship with God that was just beginning (Genesis 3:8). Much later the prophet Isaiah said, **Your iniquities have separated between you and your God, and your sins have hid *his* face from you, that he will not hear** (Isaiah 59:2 KJV).

Adam's access to God was the source of all goodness in his life. Having sinned, Adam and Eve were placed out of reach of the tree of life and out of reach of eternal life when they were put out of the first garden. To know God is more than knowledge; it is life itself. The denial of access to the tree of life was the implicit prediction of the second death. Jesus taught his disciples about the way to restore fellowship with God when he said, **I am the way, and the truth, and the life. No one comes to the Father except through me** (John 14:6 ESV). The "Father" is God in heaven.

Nevertheless, Adam and Eve did not immediately drop dead after they sinned. When you think about it, this was strange. God had said, **for in the day that you eat of it you shall surely die** (Genesis 2:17 ESV). They were evicted from God's garden, and life under the curse became awfully hard. The curse of death was on them (Genesis 3:17). We should also remember that separation from God was a result of sin, not the punishment for it. The punishment was death and was clearly stated in Genesis 3:19.

Many years ago, I cut down a large sapling tree in autumn and it lay beside the house all winter. In the springtime the nascent buds present in the limbs still drew enough nourishment from the trunk and limbs to begin to bud with blossoms and small leaves. I marveled at the sight of it. Of course, the leaves withered and died quickly as the Spring temperatures rose. The same day I cut it down, it died, but it appeared alive for a while.

> **And the LORD God commanded the man, saying, "You may surely eat of every tree of the garden, but of the tree of the knowledge of good and evil you shall not eat, for in the day that you eat of it you shall surely die."**
> (Genesis 2:16-17 ESV).

The tree I cut down died because it was cut off from the source of life in its roots. The only possibility of future life was if a skillful tree surgeon grafted it onto a living and well rooted trunk. Its own resources would never be sufficient for self-recovery. The day the curse of death was pronounced on Adam and Eve, they were dead. The full imposition of the sentence of death on sin was prolonged so that God could provide a way of reconciliation of sinners to Himself. For more detail, see the section below, "Jesus Christ Died for Our Sins."

> ———————†———————
>
> The sentence of death on sin was prolonged so that God could provide a way of reconciliation of sinners to Himself.

THE CURSE OF DEATH

The nature of the curse on Adam's sin was more than simply a condemnation to capital punishment (death of the body). Certainly, Adam's sin resulted in God's curse of physical death. That meant he would return to the lifeless dust from which his body was formed. That aspect is primary, but not all inclusive. The curse as pronounced upon Adam flowed into all areas of the creation under Adam's authority.

Most translations of Genesis 1:28 use the words "have dominion" or "rule over" to describe the mandate God gave to Adam. **And God blessed them. And God said to them, "Be** fruitful and multiply and fill the earth and subdue it, and have dominion over the fish of the sea and over the birds of the heavens and over every living thing that moves on the earth" (Genesis 1:28 ESV). The importance of this authority given to Adam was shown by the word "dominion" repeated twice (Genesis 1:26,28).

Why are we plagued with death today? Paul identified the scope of the curse as "the whole creation." **And we know that the whole creation groans and travails in pain together until now** (Romans 8:20-22 MKJV). He calls death a "bondage to corruption." Will death ever lose its hold on us? God was and is not content with this outcome. Paul was confident in God's plan as a remedy. **For the creation was not willingly subjected to vanity, but because of Him who subjected *it* on hope that the creation itself also shall be delivered from the bondage of corruption into the glorious liberty of the children of God** (Romans 8:20,21 MKJV). Although God was righteous to judge sin, He could also be merciful to provide a remedy. Paul wrote that God imposed the necessary punishment with the hope of a permanent solution that would restore us to fellowship with Himself.

God was not obligated to detail all the ways Adam's sin affected the cosmos in the brief introduction of the book of Genesis. Genesis 3 highlighted only a few significant areas of the curse. The serpent was cursed first. In Revelation 20 the terms "dragon, satan, devil, and old serpent" are synonyms. Whether this serpent was personally the devil or a proxy (Matthew 16:23), the words of God prophesied a cosmic conflict between the church of Jesus and the powers of hell. **And I tell you, you are Peter, and on this rock I will build my church, and the gates of hell shall not prevail against it** (Matthew 16:18 ESV). This is the age-long battle of good versus evil. Not surprisingly, this is the same subject as the name of the tree, the tree of knowledge of good and evil. This conflict of good and evil has endured for hundreds of generations.

Secondly, the woman was cursed in the fulfillment of her primary role as mother, and then also in her relationship with the man. Just as the man's labor was cursed, so will her life's work become painful and hard.

Thirdly, the man was also cursed regarding the primary area of his labor, provisioning the family. Not only will his labor become painful and intensive, but whenever he picks weeds, brakes sod, or plants seed, God was reminding him he was going back to that cursed, hard ground as dust when he died. God said, **The ground is cursed because of you** (Genesis 3:17). The world order was altered when the curse of death was pronounced on Man.

THE MEANING OF CURSE

I have used the word "curse" often without explanation so far. Perhaps the meaning is unclear. The common definition is speaking evil to someone. In the Bible, a "curse" is also a judgment of harsh consequences imposed as an unpleasant penalty. The word "curse" can refer to a righteous penalty, which is different from most English usage today. Where God was involved, the word "curse" described the harsh outcome due to an individual or a community for not living in the will of God. Perpetual consequences came in nature and in strife between persons that endured for ages.

The evil is said to come from God, but it is better to understand evil as the withdrawal of God's blessing and protection, just as darkness is the withdrawal of light. Evil comes to us when we are separated from the life of God by our sin, whatever form the separation might take. Jesus taught that the curse would extend to eternal punishment if a person "died in their sins," that is, unreconciled to God.

The fallout of the curse on Man was a loss of personal contact with God. After Adam and Eve were forced out of God's garden, there was no further mention of daily contact with

God as before. God became distant. Centuries later, Abraham's revelations were years apart, the Hebrew people endured generations of slavery in Egypt, and God appeared to the nation in the wilderness as a pillar of cloud and fire. Only Moses tasted the personal presence of God "face to face" later in his life (Exodus 30:11). Violence and pride flourished in the world. The personal presence of God was rare.

As time passed, Genesis recorded that the world became a hellhole because of sin until God could stand it no longer. **And GOD saw that the wickedness of man *was* great in the earth, and *that* every imagination of the thoughts of his heart *was* only evil continually. And it repented the LORD that he had made man on the earth, and it grieved him at his heart** (Genesis 6:5-6 KJV). Although by the biblical chronology Adam lived hundreds of years, few people were found who sought fellowship with God as he had experienced. Humankind without God became toxic because God's goodness was ignored, selfishness was exalted, and the death that entered through Adam's sin came upon all persons. In the New Testament Paul referred to this increasing godlessness when he wrote, **Because, knowing God, they did not glorify Him as God, neither were thankful. But they became vain in their imaginations, and their foolish heart was darkened** (Romans 1:21 MKJV).

OTHER EFFECTS OF THE CURSE

The abundance of God's garden was forfeited because of the curse. Adam could no longer tend what grew of itself (Genesis 2:8,9). He was forced to face scarcity and a greatly increased workload. The curse of death expanded with collateral damage to life expectancy, social upheaval, cultural divisions, distrust, and violence. Within a few hundred years God said that the thoughts of Man were continually evil (Genesis 6:5). The average length of life decreased steadily after the great flood of Noah, perhaps due to climate changes, finally stabilizing in the time of Moses to seventy or eighty years (Psalm 90:10). Even with the best living conditions, this is true today, 3500 years later.

The curse of death also affected human psychology. Life became more desperate for meaning as sin corrupted human creativity in the arts and sciences. The craftiness of the serpent, who is the devil, was perfecting evil. Without the worship of the true God idolatry increased, false religion flourished, and the devil worked behind the images of idols to enslave humanity with false signs and wonders. Demonic oppression abounded.

Jesus laid blame for evil squarely on the devil when he taught that he comes to kill, to steal, and to destroy (John 10:10). He also called the devil the father of lies (John 8:44). Although Adam's and Eve's sins were counted as personal rebellion against God, they were not without the temptations of the devil who amplified selfish desires to increase sinning. Therefore, the serpent was included in God's original curse. The devil corrupts good morals like all bad company does, coloring all desires with selfishness. He was cursed to ultimate failure and humiliating defeat at the feet of the people he deceived (Genesis 3:15, Matthew 16:16-18, Revelation 20:2).

Humanity in their separation from God suffers from the curse in another way also. A mind devoid of God is locked into endless futility. This is a living death. The apostle Paul wrote, **Because that, when they knew God, they glorified *him* not as God, neither were thankful; but became vain in their imagina0tions, and their foolish heart was darkened** (Romans 1:21 KJV). And again, **Now this I say and testify in the Lord, that you must no longer walk as the Gentiles do, in the futility of their minds** (Ephesians 4:17 ESV). The futility of life without God is the theme of the Old Testament book of Ecclesiastes. Interestingly, in that book it is the surety of death that causes the frustration with life.

I watched a video lecture recently on the latest theorization of the origin of the universe. Although "Origins" was the advertised subject, the substance of the lecture never got back to true origins but only to near the beginning of the "Big Bang." One would think that the beginning of all material substances that exist is a relevant topic when discussing the origin of the Big Bang. Science gives the impression of explaining every-thing, but carefully excludes subjects it cannot explain, like how "something" can arise out of "nothing."

Sadly, "science" as it often applied is never purely a pre-sentation of facts alone but requires logical formulation within a human mind. This process allows for prejudice, favoritism, pride, and choice to enter and influence conclusions. Recently, the Higgs-Boson particle was finally found decades after its postulated existence, with much fanfare. Its existence was theorized based on behaviors of particles already discovered. By the same reasoning, creationist scientists postulate the existence of a creator based upon what was created but they are ostracized and called unscientific! When they point out genome complexity and fixity of species, rightly rejecting abio-genesis, they are correct to say the present state of the uni-verse postulates a creator.

The universe practically screams "Creator!" by virtue of its size, the irreducible complexity of life and the inherent bal-ances in nature. Is there any alternative theory for the origin of matter besides a creator? Without the axiom of a creator, futility reigns in cosmology, and most scientists continue to ignore some of the most basic questions of life: personality, spirituality, logical reasoning, emotions, and love.

IS DEATH GOING TO PREVAIL?

The opposite of origin is destiny. The influence of the reality of death can be seen in the predictions of scientists. Scientists without faith in God will agree that the only destined outcome of the current expanding universe is cold, silent death. The curse of death has them spellbound and hopeless. Their best hope is that individual death will swallow them quickly before the slow agonizing winding down of the universe. People react to hope-lessness on two extremes. Some live with love, and some with total abandonment to selfishness. Both are doing as they please but arrive at such different lifestyles from the same "facts."

To an atheist, destiny is a dissolution into non-sentient non-existence. This is as "blissful" as life gets. Physically speaking, the current scientific expectation of the dissolution of everything into space dust is tantamount to an admission that God's curse of "dust to dust" is true! For them this is a preferable end because at least there is no anticipation of a face-to-face meeting with God.

God gives us hope that this is *not* our destiny if we will respond to him in repentance and faith before we die. The best ending we can imagine for our physical universe must be the end of death. This is what God has planned.

A GLIMMER OF HOPE

Adam and Eve experienced life as a slow death after their sin. The Hebrew of Genesis 2:17 translated "surely die" is a repetition of the word "to die." In effect, God was saying, Dying you will die. Doubling the word made it emphatic that death was bad. God's grace had already planned a redemption for sin because the imposition of a slow death gave Him time to work out the redemption from that death. God encoded a clue to this plan within the words He used when He cursed the serpent.

> **The LORD God said to the serpent, "Because you have done this, cursed are you above all livestock and above all beasts of the field; on your belly you shall go, and dust you shall eat all the days of your life. I will put enmity between you and the woman, and between your offspring and her offspring; he shall bruise your head, and you shall bruise his heel.**
> Genesis 3:14-15 ESV.

In this simple prophecy, God speaks of conflict down through the generations. The Bible from Moses's Genesis to John's Revelation reveals divine design that progresses as a divine plan toward a final judgment where death itself will be defeated. Meanwhile, God offers the possibility of individual redemption within the lifetime of a person. There is purpose in the long-range plan, and also within a single lifetime. The plan stretches from Genesis to Revelation, but each person can seek reconciliation with God before they die within their own lifetime.

> The Bible from Moses's Genesis to John's Revelation reveals divine design that progresses as a divine plan toward a final judgment

Some people like to use the word "evolution" to describe the earth's timeline. A better perspective is to give credit to the divine imperative will of the Creator. **For thus says the LORD, who created the heavens (he is God!), who formed the earth and made it (he established it; he did not create it empty, he formed it to be inhabited!): "I am the LORD, and there is no other."** Isaiah 45:18 ESV.

Evolution, as a theory, is merely a sum of chance processes, and there is "no chance" that biological and botanical life arrived at its current complexity and balance through genetic mutation. My mother always taught me, "Two wrongs don't make a right." How then can billions of "wrongs" in gene sequencing produce intensely inter-dependent biological life processes in an animal, or between mutually dependent separate organisms in a balanced ecosystem? And if you do not believe my mom, mathematicians say the odds are impossible. Geneticists say the mutations in a well-functioning organic life-form have more probability of causing adverse results than any increase in viability.

Some people's "Science" only allows for evolution because they have excluded the possibility of God. They say, "It is a long shot, but we will find how it was possible. God did not create everything because there is no God." I guess if a person denies the existence of the number four, then there are an infinite number of *wrong* answers for x in the formula "*2+2=x*". In your lifetime you will not get through all the infinite possibilities of wrong answers, so do not try it. Just admit "4" exists and you are done. When it comes to creation, God is the obvious answer.

Once I was telling a college woman about the truth of Christianity, but she said she could not accept that without learning about all the other religions in the world. Life is not long enough to do that! Rather, what we see on earth among created things is like a billboard announcing "God at Work," personally and progressively. In the Bible, God takes credit for creation; so, believe Him. God only gives you one life to figure this out. Why not accept the one correct answer for the wonders of life staring you in the face while you are young, and get on with life?

Death in nature appears undefeatable. Is there hope for redemption from this evil? Yes. Paul said God will redeem the whole creation (Romans 8:21). But humanity must also acknowledge that human sin today is a primary cause of perverting nature and breeding death.

If many of the imbalances in nature are created by humans, why can we not just call that sin like God does? People say diseases are not a result of sin, but rich governments spend millions on biolabs making existing diseases more deadly. Then toxins are released from the labs, whether by accident or on purpose, and the evil is done. Where does the blame lie? **The heart is deceitful above all things, and desperately sick; who can understand it?** (Jeremiah 17:9 ESV).

An ocean polluted with plastic waste is rooted in simple greed, laziness, and selfishness. If we can send people to the moon and back, we can figure out the science of waste disposal! How much research and expense are going into rocket ships to Mars? Have we made any improvements to the Moon in the fifty years since we went there? We managed to leave garbage there, I know. Beyond that I am not sure of the benefits. The root of so many problems is defective human will.

No one has found a cure for a diseased will except God. God has the answers for sin in his plan. His plan is revealed in the Bible and is a glimmer of hope for us. What about you? Can you say that you want His answer in your life? Is your will diseased or healthy? An individual cannot use the excuse of widespread natural evil to avoid their guilt for the evil they do. God challenges us to deal with the evil in our own lives first and leave the rest to Him.

WHEN DID DEATH BEGIN?

The curse of death, although occurring in stages, is one curse (Genesis 2:16,17). The judgment was assured as soon as Adam sinned. This is what God meant when he said, **for in the day that you eat of it you shall surely die**. We could compare this to a conviction at a judicial trial.

The penalty for sin was the curse of death. From man's viewpoint death included the loss of physical life, exclusion from fellowship with God, the loss of productivity in the soil, broken human relationships, eternal separation from God who is life, and defeat by the devil. From God's viewpoint He was giving sin a proper rebuttal as the rebellion that it is and was setting in motion an eventual purification of the universe by fire (2 Peter 3:7). However, because God chose to impose the penalty incrementally, it allowed time for repentance in men and women to find the grace offered by God before they died.

God in mercy did not immediately enforce a final punishment on our spirit or flesh. After the first sin, He judged the earth and banned Adam and Eve from the garden of God. God instituted a lifespan for mankind who now came under the inevitable decay of death. Scientists agree that the universe is in a slow death spiral, and many decry the decay of societal morals while fearing the self-destruction of humanity. Paul called this "a bondage of corruption" (Romans 8:21). But the delay in a final judgment for death allowed God to provide a way of escape from the curse through the sacrifice of a righteous substitute, who is Jesus Christ. Paul called this process of delay in a final judgment a "subjection in hope" in Romans 8:20, or an "over-looking" of past sins. Peter called the delay "God's longsuffering" (2 Peter 3:3).

THE SECOND DEATH

From the day sin entered the world, God set a time for a final judgment at the end of the age for a final sentencing on humankind for sin. The event is named from John's prophetic words in Revelation 20:11 as the "great white throne judgment." God calls the result of this sentencing hearing in the future "the second death."

Seeing only the first death of the body, most people are in terrifying blindness of the second death God has in store for all who "die in their sins" (John 8:24). The apostle Paul taught that the resurrected Jesus will be the judge over the whole earth on a future day. Peter said the same (Acts 10:42). Those who have passed away will be resurrected to judgment. The only escape from condemnation is to call upon God for forgiveness now, before death, and put personal faith in Jesus as the Savior (Acts 17:22-34). No matter how much one believes in eternal "non-existence" the shocking reality of God's eternity will be evident one second after physical death.

God in mercy invites everyone to come to him for the gift of eternal life. We do not approach God trusting in self-promotion. God judges us for our sins, not for our good works. An organized crime hitman indicted for murder is not excused because he loved his wife and children. He goes to trial because he is a murderer. When you think about it, a person who claims mercy based on doing only a few good works is self-incriminating. Why did he not do good all the time?

God is concerned with the good and evil in the world. Many people complain that it is God's fault when they see the injustices and sufferings of life. In part, they are complaining that this life is unfair, assuming that this life is all that there is. God agrees that this life is unfair. That is why all the injustices and inequities of life are to be settled in this world *and* in the world to come. God will bring justice to every life and has declared there will be a final judgment.

When we discuss the revelation of "the second death," then the greater plan of God's justice comes into focus. Jesus told a story about a rich man and a beggar named Lazarus, who begged at his gate. The story began in this life but they both died, and their relationship continued after their deaths when their roles were reversed. **But Abraham said, 'Child, remember that you in your lifetime received your good things, and Lazarus in like manner bad things; but now he is comforted here, and you are in anguish'** (Luke 16:25 ESV). Jesus was well aware of the injustices of life in this world, and he was teaching that God will deal with them in the fuller context of this life and the life to come.

The significant revelations of the Scriptures are that there is a life to come after death, and that there is another death to come after bodily death. Jesus came to give us life. He taught, **The thief comes only to steal and kill and destroy. I came that they may have life and have it abundantly. I am the good shepherd. The good shepherd lays down his life for the sheep** (John 10:10-11 ESV). The abundant life he taught about was a life that is beyond what most people think is possible: "eternal life." In opposition to life, there is a second death that is worse than the first. Jesus said he came to save the lost and deliver us from the second death that is coming at the last and great judgment of God.

A PLAN FOR PARDON

Here is the ancient mystery now revealed: God has fixed a date in the future to pronounce a sentence of "second death" on sinners (Acts 17:31). This is called the great white throne judgment.

> **And I saw a great white throne, and him that sat on it, from whose face the earth and the heaven fled away; and there was found no place for them. And I saw the dead, small and great, stand before God; and the books were opened: and another book was opened, which is *the book* of life: and the dead were judged out of those things which were written in the books, according to their works.**
>
> Revelation 20:11-12 KJV.

The first phase of death is the slow death of living through life on earth, growing older, and dying by degrees until we physically expire. Of course, there are many ways to die younger also. All death is a part of the curse, whatever cause. Adam, Eve and all their descendants are sentenced to this judgment.

The second phase of death is the final judgment, which is called the second death. This is not implemented until after a trial at the end of the age (Matthew 25:41). The delay in sentencing and implementation of the second death allows God to maintain divine order over the world *with justice*, giving time and opportunity for repentance towards God and faith in Jesus Christ, **whom God put forward as a propitiation by his blood, to be received by faith. This was to show God's righteousness, because in his divine forbearance he had passed over former sins** (Romans 3:25 ESV).

God's justice had delayed punishment on past sins because of the future sufficiency of the sacrifice of Christ in death at the cross. In other words, the payment for sins by the single death of Christ covered all sins before and after the historical death of Christ. In addition to forgiveness of past sins, the believer is given exemption from a future eternal punishment when he or she believes in Jesus who is raised from the dead.

God is waiting for our personal response of faith in Jesus as the unique Son of God and Savior. The supreme sacrifice of Jesus is sufficient for all who ask for forgiveness, and the invitation found in many verses is given to a universal group of "whosoever is willing may come." We connect with God by our faith. When Paul wrote, we are "justified by faith" (Romans 5:1) it is clear by what was already quoted that faith is a condition of personally receiving the objective "propitiation by his blood." Our faith is based on a real physical death, given as a substitute for sinners. Therefore, God is glorified for being the gracious provider of our forgiveness.

Part 2

God's Remedy for Death is Jesus Christ

It will be said on that day, "Behold, this is our God; we have waited for him, that he might save us. This is the LORD; we have waited for him; let us be glad and rejoice in his salvation."

Isaiah 25:9 ESV

The Curse for Sin is Death

Adam's sin brought the judgment of death into the world. Paul taught this plainly enough, but we have failed to understand it. **Therefore, just as sin came into the world through one man, and death through sin, and so death spread to all men because all sinned** (Romans 5:12 ESV).

Where there is a failure to understand that death is the result of sin, then the death of Jesus Christ will be misunderstood. *The death of Jesus is viewed by most people as a normal death, when in fact it was the most unjust outcome in God's creation for a man who lived a perfect life.* It was utterly impossible in a just universe for God to let that happen. If He was so concerned with the punishment of sin that He gave the death sentence to Adam, then He must be equally zealous (in accord with his righteousness) to reward a perfect life. In truth the death of Jesus Christ was a sacrifice made possible *only* when Jesus willingly offered himself, and *only* when God his Father received it as a substitutionary offering for others in love.

> Where there is a failure to understand that death is the result of sin, then the death of Jesus Christ will be misunderstood.

Physical death is the end of life on earth, the end of all a person's hopes and dreams and plans. It is the finality of the end of life that causes the preacher in the Old Testament wisdom book of Ecclesiastes to cry out, **A person who has toiled with wisdom and knowledge and skill must leave everything to be enjoyed by someone who did not toil for it. This also is vanity and a great evil!** (Ecclesiastes 2:21).

And worse still is when a person dies in this life unreconciled to God because the curse of death follows him to the next life. A human being was designed in God's image, a blending of spirit and flesh (Genesis 1:27, 2:4). Jesus said that dying unforgiven is "dying in your sins." **He said to them, "You are from below; I am from above. You are of this world; I am not of this world. I told you that you would die in your sins, for unless you believe that I am he you will die in your sins"** (John 8:23-24 ESV).

The "he" Jesus is referring to is himself, the promised Messiah of Israel. Messiah was revealed by Isaiah the prophet as the one who would "bear the sins of many" (Isaiah 53:6). To "bear sins" of others meant the Savior accepted their guilt so that their punishment fell on the sinner's substitute. The phrase "to bear their sin" did not mean Messiah would be a bucket into which "sin" was poured. This is because "sin" is not an object, but a wicked deed done by a person. Without a substitute to bear the punishment for sin, every person was left to bear the punishment of their own sins. This meant they would "die with their sin unforgiven" and proceed to the second death.

There was no way to avoid the curse of death in this world or out of this world. God spoke it to Adam, and it has happened (Genesis 3:19). We all die. This well-known curse said, "created from dust, to dust you shall return." It is sometimes repeated at funerals. This is the first death. Without a reconciliation with God, the sinner is still not home free, even if he dies. His sins remain unforgiven, for the judgment of the second death is based upon the works of this physical life (Revelation 20:12).

God never said the death of a sinner is redemptive. God never told Adam that after he died, he would be good with God again. His death was a punishment only, not a basis of forgiveness or reconciliation. Only the life of Christ and his perfections are sufficient basis to pay the price of our forgiveness and bring redemption (Revelation 5:1-5).

Our only recourse is to personally repent for our sins, believe in Jesus, and receive his exemption from the judgment to come. Having trusted

———✝———

Having trusted in Christ, he has united us to himself, and our entire experience with death began to change.

in Christ, he has united us to himself, and our entire experience with death began to change. **There is therefore now no condemnation for those who are in Christ Jesus. For the law of the Spirit of life has set you free in Christ Jesus from the law of sin and death** (Romans 8:1-2 ESV). Sin and death are so omnipresent as to be called a "law" of life. Yet Paul wrote that the Spirit of life in Christ Jesus has the power to set us free. Forgiveness in Jesus is a higher law than punishment. It is the gift of life itself.

THE CURSE AS PHYSICAL DEATH

The curse of death given to Adam in Genesis 3 describes physical death: **In the sweat of your face you shall eat bread until you return to the ground, for out of it you were taken. For dust you *are*, and to dust you shall return** (Genesis 3:19 MKJV). This death is physical with no mention of eternal punishment.

The initial warning of God was that disobedience will bring death. **But you shall not eat of the tree of knowledge of good and evil. For in the day that you eat of it you shall surely die** (Genesis 2:17 MKJV). We know from Genesis that when God said death would come the "same day" as disobedience occurred, that God meant the curse of death would be imposed on that day. It was. The curse, however, had many parts including physical death, the spread of death throughout creation, broken relationships, and finally the second death judgment for eternity. The meaning of the curse unfolded only after God pronounced to Adam that he would return to dust.

Physical death was possible by the creation of the human body in the temporal and non-eternal physical universe. Man was made of dirt, the physical stuff, even though he was simultaneously endowed with the life-force of God, which we call spirit. He made mankind from the beginning in a physical world.

When God pronounced the curse on Adam, he judged Adam and Eve as newly created physical beings. As far as we know, they had no comprehension of the spiritual dimension at the beginning. He walked in the garden to meet them. They did not pray, but just talked to God. This is how we grow from our own infancy, bound to physical reality and only gradually understanding spiritual realities.

At the first judgment for sin, God told them they would die and return to the dust from which they were made. That was bad news. They were about to meet the curse of death on many levels. Only as time passed would they become aware of the spiritual and eternal aspects of death included in the original curse. Surely the horror of human death was felt at the death of their son Abel; but that was years later. The deeper meaning of death grew with their experiences and further divine revelation.

The lack of mention of eternal punishment in Genesis 3 showed that God wanted humanity to get the message of the seriousness of sin beginning on a physical level.

The horror of physical death was awful. It was then and has been ever since. Physical death was God's judgment on sin, and the lack of mention of eternal punishment in Genesis 3 showed that God wanted humanity to get the message of the seriousness of sin beginning on a physical level.

If God imposed death as a punishment, then it was not part of his "very good" Creation as original equipment. When it is understood that death is not normal, it prompts the bigger question "How can I be forgiven to avoid death?" As history progressed, humanity experienced the devastating effects of physical death, and was better prepared to understand the even worse "second death" of

When it is understood that death is not normal, it prompts the bigger question "How can I be forgiven to avoid death?"

eternal punishment when they heard the gospel. If physical death is as bad as we know it is by experience, then the prospect of a final judgment and eternal punishment called the

---†---

The delay in sentencing and implementation of the second death allows God to maintain divine order over the world with justice.

---

second death, is almost incomprehensible. This was and continues to be the basis of the fear of God.

Biblical revelation discloses death as a many headed beast. The subject of death is divided by God in Scripture into two parts: physical death and the second death. If these deaths are separated by God in the timeline of world history, it is not unreasonable to understand them as distinct in soteriology (the study of redemption). Physical death in the world becomes our first experience with the seriousness of life. The shallowness of a "You only live once" philosophy is devastated by the revelation of dying twice.

God first pronounced physical death as a punishment for sin, but then employed it as a wakeup call for all persons to seek reconciliation with God before an even worse unfolding of death arrives. Physical death was specified by God as the punishment of Adam's sin in Genesis 3, and the expulsion from the garden that separated them from the tree of life foreshadowed the final judgment of the second death of eternal punishment.

A silver lining in the original curse was that death came only at the end of a lifetime. God was assigning the punishment for sin in a righteous manner, but a delayed process allowed for a sinner's repentance and reconciliation with God, if the right process could be found.

A Plan for Redemption

The plan of redemption as revealed in the Scriptures has been the faint light at the end of the tunnel for those who hope in God while awaiting the work of remediation. The introduction of sin against God into the world put God in an awful situation (humanly speaking), namely, whether to banish mankind forever, or let the disobedience slide, thereby denying His own justice, goodness, and perfection. Of course, He knew what He would do.

Here is a key revelation: The full judgment of death for sinning was not imposed immediately on Adam and Eve, allowing God to provide a way of reconciliation of sinners to Himself. The first sin did not end all life immediately, which is what might be expected when death is the penalty. Death entered the world in Genesis 3, and the countdown to the final judgment began.

Since the time of Adam and Eve a general distribution of God's grace has sustained the world. Jesus taught, **But I say to you, Love your enemies and pray for those who persecute you, so that you may be sons of your Father who is in heaven. For he makes his sun rise on the evil and on the good, and sends rain on the just and on the unjust** (Matthew 5:44-45 ESV).

Right from the beginning, the infinite wisdom of God had all the contingencies covered for the success of His original intention for fellowship with the humans He made. By providing a way of forgiveness that meets His standard of justice in punishing sin, God made forgiveness available to all who repent and believe in God. Redemption is founded upon the life, death, and resurrection of Jesus Christ, God's unique Son.

The first Adam brought sin and its punishment of death into the world. Jesus is the "last Adam," the new start for all mankind. His purpose was to fix what the first Adam had broken. **For as in Adam all die, even so in Christ shall all be made alive** (1 Corinthians 15:22 KJV). His mission was to correct the evil outcome of the first Adam who led us into sinful behavior. When we repent and believe in Jesus, God returns us to the path of His original intent when He created the world.

DEATH BY DEGREES

Death in Scripture has levels of meaning. In Genesis 3 Adam and Eve were sentenced with death. The primary meaning is *physical death* in Genesis 3. Traditionally this is called "the curse," but this was a righteous judgment for sin. The curse of death is when our bodies return to the dust of the ground from which we were made (Genesis 3:19). Physical death was a terrible price to pay for sin because God designed us for the enjoyment of life's physical pleasures. Add to that loss the psychological pain of unrealized hopes, lost dreams, and failed love. Each of those is a kind of death while we are alive. God included the warning that strife would grow between the man and his wife, too. Watching the physical end of life around us throttles our spirits with discouragement.

Of course, God did not make us as merely physical. I think some school children still get the assignment to write an essay on the subject "Why I am worth more than $4.99 of chemicals." I am so old that when I was in school the assignment was "Why I am worth more than 99 cents." The point is that the spirit of man presupposes meaning in life beyond the physical body, so that death itself has a deeper meaning than physical death and a return to dust. The curse of death begins with physical death but extends to a second death which is eternal punishment from God (Mark 9:48). All these meanings were in the warning of God to Adam that sin would bring death, even if Adam's understanding was limited at the first.

The result of dying unforgiven in this physical life is being locked into a legal condemnation to a *second death*. **But as for the cowardly, the faithless, the detestable, as for murderers, the sexually immoral, sorcerers, idolaters, and all liars, their portion will be in the lake that burns with fire and sulfur, which is the second death** (Revelation 21:8 ESV). If there is one thought that will drive an individual atheist to his knees, it is the desire to pray that there is no God who will judge his life in the afterlife. When he realizes the irony of the situation, he might as well repent since he is already on his knees!

The scriptural revelation in Genesis was that death is a legal judgment (curse) pronounced upon Adam and Eve for their sin of disobedience. God held Adam legally responsible because the warning not to eat of the tree was given to him directly (Genesis 2:16-17). The death sentence was sure, but it did not result in the immediate loss of life for Adam and Eve. It was pronounced immediately but implemented incrementally. The curse of death started with mankind being thrown out of God's garden into a world simultaneously subjected to the curse of destruction and death on man's account (Genesis 3:17). It continued with the death of the body returning to dust (soil of the ground) when they died. For Adam this occurred 930 years later. But death did not end there. A final judgment of all people who have ever lived is planned in the future.

> **The times of ignorance God overlooked, but now he commands all people everywhere to repent, because he has fixed a day on which he will judge the world in righteousness by a man whom he has appointed; and of this he has given assurance to all by raising him from the dead.** Acts 17:30-31 ESV.

Few people remember that a promise of resurrection was given to everyone who has ever lived. **Do not marvel at this, for an hour is coming when all who are in the tombs will hear his voice and come out, those who have done good to the resurrection of life, and those who have done evil to the resurrection of judgment** (John 5:28-29 ESV). This was what Jesus taught.

The two deaths are connected in unbelievers. If a person dies physically before they repent and believe in Jesus, they will be resurrected to face the great white throne judgment without hope of pardon. The second death is clearly revealed in the divine timeline of scriptural prophecy as the penalty judgment assigned to those who sinned before they died and remained unrepentant. Condemnation to the second death is enforced at this last event of judgment and is certain for unrepentant persons.

The curse of physical death has become the time limit for every person to repent. **And just as it is appointed for man to die once, and after that comes judgment...** (Hebrews 9:27 ESV). Grace is amazing, but it is only available for a limited time because a person must repent before death.

Most Christians are aware of this verse in Hebrews, but they may not realize the time between physical death and the final judgment may be thousands of years, depending on when the person lived on earth. Paul taught that the great white throne judgment is a single "appointed day" in the future for all humanity (Acts 17:31). Conviction at that judgment initiates the second death. This is also called eternal punishment and is the only possible outcome for those who "die in their sins" (John 8:24).

All the stages of the curse of death work together. Those who do not seek the pardon that comes from God are *currently* under condemnation of the curse of death. No one can hope that they will be acquitted at the final judgment. The curse of physical death is in force and should remind all persons of the impending second death, for both deaths are parts of one curse.

> **For God did not send his Son into the world to condemn the world, but in order that the world might be saved through him. Whoever believes in him is not condemned, but whoever does not believe is condemned already, because he has not believed in the name of the only Son of God.** John 3:17-18 ESV.

GOD HAD A PLAN

God had a better plan than immediately killing Adam for his disobedience. God condemned Adam on the day of his sin but set future deadlines of the first and second deaths for the fulfillment of His justice. This plan for Adam, and us, allowed time for God to provide a way for redemption of individuals *before* they die. By this plan, generations to come could experience his mercy and glorify Him for it (Exodus 34:6,7). The timing of the first and second deaths allowed Adam and Eve time to be reconciled to God before physical death. The same time interval benefits us also. We can be forgiven with the assurance of eternal life before we die.

The delay in final judgment is like a bank that has notified a homeowner that the mortgage note is in default due to non-payment. The homeowner knows they will have to leave the house when the foreclosure is finalized, but they are still living there. God has allowed the people of the world to live out their lives under condemnation for their sins without the privilege of personal friendship with God. After Adam's sin "death reigned" over all people (Romans 5:14), but not without hope of divine intervention and redemption.

God has allowed a delay in the imposition of the first death sentence so that we may have the opportunity to find Him. That delay is the length of days before physical death. As Paul preached in Athens,

And he made from one man every nation of mankind to live on all the face of the earth, having determined allotted periods and the boundaries of their dwelling place, that they should seek God, and perhaps feel their way toward him and find him. Yet he is actually not far from each one of us. Acts 17:26-27 ESV.

This is how Isaiah also preached our current lost state: ...**but your iniquities have made a separation between you and your God, and your sins have hidden his face from you so that he does not hear** (Isaiah 59:2 ESV).

There is little detail written about Adam's personal faith during his life. Genesis supplies personalized accounts of faith beginning with Abraham (Genesis 12 onward). Before Jesus came there was a place for repentance and a relationship with God by faith, but after Jesus lived on earth the promises were much more clearly understood.

Paul rightly understood that the grace of God was effective before the incarnation of Jesus in history because Abraham believed God's promise and was justified before God. He was justified through faith in God's promises of forgiveness, although the death of Jesus was future and not yet revealed. **For what does the Scripture say? "Abraham believed God, and it was counted to him as righteousness"** (Romans 4:3 ESV). By faith in God's promise, Abraham was credited with the righteousness of Jesus long before Jesus came.

It was Paul's privilege, which is also handed down to us, to proclaim the manifestation of the grace of God in Jesus. **But when the fullness of time had come, God sent forth his Son, born of woman, born under the law, to redeem those who were under the law, so that we might receive adoption as sons** (Galatians 4:4-5 ESV). Paul was preaching the love of God completed on a Roman cross in Jerusalem, whereas Abraham had to believe the words of God as a promise. We follow in the steps of "the faith of Abraham, who is the father of us all" (Romans 4:16 KJV). As Abraham believed the promises of God, we believe that **...which we have heard, which we have seen with our eyes, which we have looked upon, and our hands have handled, of the Word of life** (1 John 1:1 KJV).

Salvation is dependent upon our personal repentance to God for our sins. Many people saw Jesus and his works but remained hard hearted (John 15:24). Like Abraham, we are required to put our faith to work, believing in Messiah Jesus, who laid down his life for us.

People take offense at the thought of repentance because experience has shown us that admitting our faults was a weakness that allowed others to gain an advantage over us. We must humbly acknowledge that God always has had the advantage over us, but He does not act like sinful people. His forgiveness is freely given and can be the fresh start in life we have wanted all along. Jesus said that he is "gentle and lowly in heart," so he will not take advantage of us in our broken-hearted condition. He does not hold the guilt of our sins over us, as if he were extorting us. He offers us a full pardon at his own expense.

Jesus said, **Truly, truly, I say to you, whoever hears my word and believes him who sent me has eternal life. He does not come into judgment, but has passed from death to life** (John 5:24 ESV). The new spiritual birth of repentance and faith in Jesus removes our condemnation. Jesus takes upon himself the guilt of sinners. He bears the burden of guilt on our behalf by his death on the cross. Through the forgiveness of sins there is a full redemption from the sentence of death given to Adam.

God pronounced in a judicial sentence that Adam's body would return to dust (Genesis 3:17-19). Later revelation has taught us that this sentence of death on Adam had an eternal consequence also. Death had an initial effect of corruption of the body when it returned to dust, but Man's spirit and resurrected body will be condemned to a "second death" after the death of the body. God did not design humankind to be only physical because personal consciousness continues past the death of the body. Our spirit returns to God who made us to await a final judgment (Ecclesiastes 12:7). A final judgment will be a non-ending experience of death in torments, separated from the presence of God.

All that is currently good in the earth is an extension of God's grace to give us time to repent. When we talk about God's plan for the world, death was the central problem that required a solution. Death can be experienced in different dimensions because God has created us as spirit and body creatures. The first death is cessation of life in the body. The second death is eternal punishment. These are scripturally defined. Jesus said, **And do not fear those who kill the body but cannot kill the soul. Rather fear him who can destroy both soul and body in hell** (Matthew 10:28 ESV).

THE GREAT DIVISION

Jesus warned us against a common religious view that life after death applies the same to all persons. Instead, he separated the dead into two groups. **Do not marvel at this, for an hour is coming when all who are in the tombs will hear his voice and come out, those who have done good to the resurrection of life, and those who have done evil to the resurrection of judgment** (John 5:28-29 ESV).

In another passage in John chapter 8, Jesus marked the division of two groups as "those who believe that I am he" (Messiah), and those who will "die in their sins" (John 8:24). Jesus said there will be a return to bodily existence for all persons, and that there will be forgiveness for some and judgment for others. The outcome of condemnation will be the "second death." The outcome of receiving forgiveness will be eternal life in the presence of God.

It is critical to understand that the atoning work of Christ is a redemption from all effects of the curse of death. Beyond physical death, the redemptive work of Jesus Christ must redeem us for all eternity. This is what God accomplished when Jesus died. A spiritual victory was secured at Calvary's cross with ever expanding effects as the gospel of Jesus is preached in the world. History is moving toward a final judgment at the end of this epoch, and the elimination of death from God's eternal kingdom.

The history of Israel and the doctrine of the first Christian apostles both show that the flow of history is following a plan of redemption and is not random. Along the way there is no instant perfection, there is no magic potion, and there is no political savior who can solve the world's problem of sin and death. As Paul wrote, **For as in Adam all die, so also in Christ shall all be made alive** (1 Corinthians 15:22 ESV). God is the only Savior.

God's remedy for the judgment of death on Adam and his descendants was the death of Jesus on the cross. This is because Jesus had no liability of death as a punishment for his own sins since he had none. The spiritual result of Jesus's death and resurrection was a substitutionary payment by death that redeemed sinners from both the first and second deaths in one physical death. **... he entered once for all into the holy places, not by means of the blood of goats and calves but by means of his own blood, thus securing an eternal redemption** (Hebrews 9:12 ESV). This is known as the doctrine of blood atonement.

Traditionally, some theologians have had difficulty explaining how the physical death of Jesus could accomplish the redemption of sinners from punishments beyond physical death, such as eternal torment in hell. However, apostolic teaching assured us that a single redemptive act at Calvary did accomplish so great a salvation. The depth and breadth of redemption is rooted in the physical life of Jesus. **But we see him who for a little while was made lower than the angels, namely Jesus, crowned with glory and honor because of the suffering of death, so that by the grace of God he might taste death for everyone** (Hebrews 2:9 ESV).

This salvation is applied around the world one convicted sinner at a time as an individual comes to a crisis of faith in Jesus. A believer then starts to grow in the knowledge of God. **But grow in the grace and knowledge of our Lord and Savior Jesus Christ. To him be the glory both now and to the day of eternity** (2 Peter 3:18 ESV). Jesus said that being born of the Spirit of God is as mysterious as the unseen wind. It is not "scientific," nor can it be initiated by human will acting in or upon another person. Salvation will not be found in saying the correct version of "the sinner's prayer," but in personal faith. **But to all who did receive him, who believed in his name, he gave the right to become children of God, who were born, not of blood nor of the will of the flesh nor of the will of man, but of God** (John 1:12-13 ESV). A cure for death that goes beyond human death is only found in God Himself.

JESUS THE SECRET KING

I do not know about you, but I do take significant pleasure in being proved right. In my case, there is surely some pride involved, so I try not to dwell on it. God, however, is pleased that his truth is known, and his justice is accomplished with righteousness. **For the word of the LORD *is* right; and all his works *are done* in truth** (Psalms 33:4 KJV). God is content to reveal his wonders at a time of his own choosing to glorify Himself. He is planning some big "reveals."

Look for instance at Psalm 2. God's reaction to the boastful rebellion of tyrants is a wry laugh. **Yet have I set my king upon my holy hill of Zion** (Psalms 2:6 KJV). The word "yet" indicates God's will prevailing against all opposition. In the terminology of sporting competitions, God always has "the momentum." The God of heaven laughs at the rebellion of an ungrateful creation because He always has the momentum of his own will.

> The God of heaven laughs at the rebellion of an ungrateful creation because He always has the momentum of his own will.

The Son-King of Psalm 2, written about a thousand years prior to our Lord's birth, is clearly a prophecy of Jesus Christ. The apostolic preaching identified Jesus as the Son-King (Hebrews 1:1–5; Acts 13:33). The apostles proclaimed God's personal rule over his creation through Messiah because of the father/son connection. Jesus said, **I and *my* Father are one** (John 10:30 KJV). On one occasion the claim of Jesus to be the Son of God elicited cries of "Blasphemy!" from his fellow Jews because the father/son connection was so revered in Israel that they knew this was a claim of divinity (John 8:59).

In Psalm 2 the reign of the Son-King is the perfect expression of the will of God in action. All opposition is "held in derision" because of the inequality of power between God and

Man. The Son-King has been set in place by the will of God. His rule is fixed and on a durable foundation.

The rule of the great King is not without opposition, however. As futile as rebellion may be, those in rebellion are allowed time and space to strut, speaking words of insurrection, and forming reinforcing coalitions. Because God has allowed time for personal repentance, they are proud, and they do not recognize that God has placed a time limit for their repentance.

Notwithstanding all boastings of the rebellious ones, the God of the Son-King laughs. The throne of the King is established. The rebellion is an exercise in futility because the Son-King need only "ask" and his enemies will be laid waste to the ends of the earth. Not a square foot of the earth is exempt from his rule. Delay is not denial, and God is patient with love and hope, giving extension of time for the gospel to be preached, and for humanity to bow the knee to Jesus.

> God is patient with love and hope, giving extension of time for the gospel to be preached, and for humanity to bow the knee to Jesus.

Ask of me, and I shall give thee the heathen for thine inheritance, and the uttermost parts of the earth for thy possession (Psalms 2:8 KJV). The world is still waiting for the word of Jesus to be voiced to ask for his manifest rule over the earth. God has His times and seasons (Acts 1:6-7). Preaching the return of Christ to rule the earth was a fundamental truth in the early gospel message (Acts 10:42).

Some people recognized Jesus as the King of heaven by the works he did, despite his normal looking flesh and blood body. Others refused to see Jesus as the secret King. A Roman captain came to Jesus seeking healing for his slave. As he spoke to Jesus about his need he said, **Speak the word only and my servant will be healed** (Matthew 8:8). Jesus answered the man's humble request. He was one who recognized spiritual authority.

JESUS LIVED IN THE SHADOW OF DEATH

Jesus was a hard man to kill. His Father in heaven always "gave his angels charge over" the well-being of the Son of God (Psalm 91:11). His earthly father Joseph was instructed twice in dreams to take specific action to protect the child. The first time Joseph was instructed to proceed to full marriage with Mary to provide a stable and safe home for Jesus, despite the embarrassment of her early pregnancy. A second time, after the birth of Jesus in Bethlehem, he was warned to flee to Egypt before King Herod in his rage killed all the infants living there.

When he began to preach in Nazareth, Jesus was dragged to the brow of a hill, ready to be thrown down. I visited there once, and it is a steep slope. But he just walked through the mob, and they parted to let him get away.

Another time, Jesus was led by the Spirit into the desert places. I am convinced by the wilderness temptation narrative that Jesus fasted to the point of death. His weakened condition required supernatural angelic help to survive, reminiscent of Elijah in his flight from Jezebel centuries earlier.

Then there was the time that their boat was ready to sink in a storm. Jesus rebuked the wind and the waves to bring a great calm. The life of Jesus was always in danger.

He also used his "sanctified common sense" to avoid exposure in politically sensitive areas. His reputation grew to exceed that of the Baptizer in Judea (John 3: 1-3). As he was led by the Spirit of God, Jesus alternately avoided politically dangerous situations or moved straight ahead into confrontation, confident of his Father's protection (Matthew 26:53).

At the appointed time Jesus appeared in Jerusalem in a holy parade before Passover, knowing full well how the confrontation would end. On a previous journey to Jerusalem Jesus righteously predicted that he would be "lifted up," a foreshadowing of his crucifixion (John 8:28, 12:32, 10:18). He taught the people that he had the authority to lay down his life and to take it up again (John 10:18).

He was always in control, even when it seemed he was not. His life was guided by the Holy Spirit so that he would arrive in Jerusalem on a precise calendar event, the annual feast of Passover. The Messiah, whom John the Baptist called the Lamb of God, died on the day that commemorated two noteworthy events: the exodus from slavery in Egypt, and the passing over of the death angel the night before the exodus. During Passover faith-filled families killed a lamb per house and applied the blood of the sacrifice to the doorframes of their homes. His crucifixion was surrounded with themes of death and deliverance from death.

After the resurrection Peter preached that God planned all the sufferings of Jesus, although wicked hands performed the crucifixion (Acts 2:23). The timing, place, and all the supporting political drama was stunningly orchestrated by a Higher Power, so that the death of Jesus fulfilled ancient prophecies.

THE MISSION OF JESUS

Jesus's mission was to end the curse of death on sinners who repent and believe in him. The penalty of the curse was primarily physical death (Genesis 3:19). I use the word "primary" meaning occurring first. This does not discount or ignore eternal punishment. Jesus dealt with the curse of physical death first because it is antecedent to the second death. Physical death began in Genesis 3, but the second death does not occur until after the Millennium (Revelation 20).

Adam died physically at the age of 930 for the sin he brought into the world. The curse of the first death is upon all persons because all have sinned. **Yet death reigned from Adam to Moses, even over those whose sinning was not like the transgression of Adam, who was a type of the one who**

was to come (Romans 5:14 ESV). The mission of Jesus was to deal with this aspect of the curse of death first.

Since everyone dies, we tend to think that physical death is a normal part of life. Death is so "normal" we do not think it has spiritual significance. Many theologians only want to talk about the spiritual aspects of death including eternal hell. Paul did not see it this way. Death came because of sin, Paul wrote, and that is why everyone has died since Adam (Romans 5:15). Death passed to all persons because Adam stood as representative of all his descendants. Besides that, every person sinned for themselves and was guilty before God. Paul said everyone decays in the grave because we all sin (whatever kind of sin does not matter). **The sting of death *is* sin; and the strength of sin *is* the law** (1 Corinthians 15:56 KJV).

But Jesus came and nailed the law to the cross (Colossians 2:14). By this word picture, Paul was teaching that the law of sin and death (Romans 8:2) no longer had a legal claim on sinners who are forgiven because of the substitutionary death of Jesus. It was like when a prosecutor is pressing charges against a criminal before a judge. But then, after he makes his case, the defense attorney shows the judge that the law was revoked. The crime was committed, but there are no current grounds for prosecution. **For sin will have no dominion over you, since you are not under law but under grace** (Romans 6:14 ESV).

Being forgiven is one way to throw off the lordship of the law of sin, but Paul also taught that sin's power is broken through the defeat of lusts and selfish desires as we consider ourselves "dead with Christ." **But thanks be to God, that you who were once slaves of sin have become obedient from the heart to the standard of teaching to which you were committed, and, having been set free from sin, have become slaves of righteousness** (Romans 6:17-18 ESV). In this way, the availability of forgiveness never becomes an excuse to sin.

In the case of Jesus, his death was a substitute for ours. The death penalty has already been paid for believers. It is as if the defense attorney showed the judge that a proper punishment has already been completed. The judge can then pronounce that the case has been properly closed. God has fast-tracked our case to conclusion on account of Jesus. Cleansing from sin seems impossible to us, but with God all things are possible.

Because every human dies, people often wrongly conclude that Jesus's death was "normal." It was not. The death of Jesus was the most *unnatural* outcome expected for a man who lived a perfect life before God. Paul explained how Jesus was not only different but was the exact opposite of Adam who sinned (Romans 5:12-21). Why then did Jesus have to die?

> The death of Jesus was the most *unnatural* outcome expected for a man who lived a perfect life before God.

If you want to understand Jesus, you must know his mission. The apostle John who was closest to his heart wrote, **And the Word became flesh and dwelt among us, and we have seen his glory, glory as of the only Son from the Father, full of grace and truth** (John 1:14 ESV). Do not just gloss over the phrase "and the Word became flesh." By using the name "Word of God" for Jesus, John is claiming the pre-existence of Jesus before he became flesh. This claim was never made for any other human in the Bible. Paul also claimed, **In him the whole fullness of deity dwells bodily** (Colossians 2:9 ESV).

Therefore, the mission of Jesus was to demonstrate by his character and deeds that he was the unique Son of God. His mission was to reveal the glory of God in a body of flesh and blood.

> Jesus decided how, when and where he would die, because he lived every day in the will of the Father.

Can God in the flesh be killed? Dying a physical death was possible because he was true flesh and blood (Hebrews 2:14). But why would Jesus have to die a physical death if the curse of death did not apply to him? The answer is that God in the flesh could not die a "normal" sinner's death. Jesus said, **For this reason the Father** loves me, because I lay down my life that I may take it up again. No one takes it from me, but I lay it down of my own accord (John 10:17-18 ESV).So the second missional purpose of Jesus was to offer his life as a sacrifice in place of sinners for the punishment of death.

"No one takes it from me," Jesus said. Jesus decided how, when and where he would die, because he lived every day in the will of the Father. He said, **And he who sent me is with me. He has not left me alone, for I always do the things that are pleasing to him** (John 8:29 ESV).

If Jesus died on purpose, then he died on a mission. He "laid down his life" to pay the penalty of death that sinners deserved. **Then Jesus, calling out with a loud voice, said, "Father, into your hands I commit my spirit!" And having said this he breathed his last** (Luke 23:46 ESV). Everyone else was under the curse of death for their own sins, but Jesus had

> If Jesus died on purpose, then he died on a mission.

none. The death of Jesus was unique, and of infinite value.

THE DEATH OF JESUS IS A BEGINNING, NOT AN ENDING

Jesus could only die in weakness. If he had stood up to fight for his life, he would have immediately won, but we would have no Savior. Therefore, he said beforehand that he would "lay down his life."

This made Jesus appear as weak and a loser. At his arrest the disciples did not understand the weakness of Jesus and how it fit into the plan of God. **Do you think that I cannot appeal to my Father, and he will at once send me more than twelve legions of angels? But how then should the Scriptures be fulfilled, that it must be so?** (Matthew 26:53-54 ESV).

Some people foolishly claim that the Father turned his back on Jesus, starting from the garden prayer until after he died. Like the disciples, they fail to understand how Jesus chose to be weak for our sakes. Obviously, Jesus knew exactly where he stood with his Father, and they agreed together that he would lay down his life in love for the lost.

The submission of Jesus to arrest was a "weakness" founded in acceptance of God's will. Thereby his own words were fulfilled that the good shepherd lays down his life for his sheep in love (John 10:11). Far from rejecting Jesus during his agony in the garden, as some preach, the Father loved him even more, if that were possible. **For this reason the Father loves me, because I lay down my life that I may take it up again** (John 10:17 ESV). The Father did not turn his back on Jesus. Jesus said his Father loved him *all the more* for laying down his life. If the Father had already rejected Jesus, as some preachers claim, a rejected man could not boast that he merely needed to ask his Father for protection from arrest to get it. Then he would have been a liar.

The rebellious only know raw power. Everything else is weakness in their sight. They see love and call it weakness. Be prepared for this taunting if you are a disciple following in his steps. Be prepared to love and not to give in to hate, even though you are mocked as weak. God told Paul, **for my strength is made perfect in weakness** (2 Corinthians 12:9). This is the mystery of God. Jesus lived this truth.

I entitled this section as "Death as a Beginning, Not an Ending." Before the crucifixion, the disciples were greatly distressed when Jesus foretold his death (Matthew 17:22-23). Jesus's death was terminal in their understanding. He was the leader, and they were nothing without him. It would be the end of their ministry. When Jesus submitted to arrest, they all abandoned him and fled (Mark 14:50). **For my thoughts are not your thoughts, neither are your ways my ways, declares the LORD. For as the heavens are higher than the earth, so are** my ways higher than your ways and my thoughts than your thoughts (Isaiah 55:8-9 ESV).

In God's plan, though, the death of Jesus was hidden wisdom. **But we speak the wisdom of God in a mystery, even the hidden wisdom, which God ordained before the world unto our glory: Which none of the princes of this world knew: for had they known it, they would not have crucified the Lord of glory** (1 Corinthians 2:7-8 KJV).

What the world called "weakness" (and still calls it weakness today when Jesus is preached) was love, because he did not have to die for his own sins, since he had none. He died for our sins, in weakness, for us to be strongly reconciled to God. **For though he was crucified through weakness, yet he lives by the power of God. For we also are weak in him, but we shall live with him by the power of God toward you** (2 Corinthians 13:4 KJV).

In Jesus Christ God made death give birth to life. This is another of those instances where everything means the opposite of what appears. Yes, indeed! The death of Jesus that was feared to mean the end of life has become the birthing event of all who were "dead in trespasses and sins" but now are made alive in Jesus Christ (Ephesians 2:4-5).

> In Jesus Christ God made death give birth to life.

RECONCILED TO GOD THROUGH JESUS'S DEATH

Paul wrote, **For if while we were enemies we were reconciled to God by the death of his Son, much more, now that we are reconciled, shall we be saved by his life** (Romans 5:10 ESV).

The fact that Jesus died for sinners before they even repented was proof for Paul that God's love was unique, overwhelming, and eternal. The grace of God leads us to repentance so that our past sins are forgiven, our present sins cleansed, and our future sins avoided.

Repentance must occur before a person's death. Being forgiven before we have died physically means our future condemnation is now removed and the ongoing divine prosecution of our sin is cancelled.

Once I was studying the history of the Bible and ran across an interesting account from about the sixteenth century. The English churches were just beginning to have the Scriptures read in the native English rather than the Latin that no one understood. Many congregants heard for the first time about the grace of God who forgives sins and they jumped up out of their seats during the public reading of the Scriptures. Certain people would shout with rejoicing or others would faint as the grace of God overwhelmed them. The churches of today are so lost in modern compromise and a multitude of humanistic words that I believe a simple return to preaching of God's love will once again overwhelm believers with the truth.

The world is full of people drowning in their guilt and impotence who need to find God. God is not holding our drowning heads under water. He sent Jesus to die for our sins so that we may be forgiven and truly begin to live. He does not bring our sins to remembrance to extort submission from us, but He revives us with abundant life.

Truly, truly, I say to you, whoever hears my word and believes him who sent me has eternal life. He does not come into judgment, but has passed from death to life. John 5:24 ESV.

For as high as the heavens are above the earth, so great is his steadfast love toward those who fear him; as far as the east is from the west, so far does he remove our transgressions from us. Psalms 103:11-12 ESV.

> For God so loved the world, that he gave his
> only Son, that whoever believes in him should
> not perish but have eternal life. For God did
> not send his Son into the world to condemn
> the world, but in order that the world might
> be saved through him. John 3:16-17 ESV.

JESUS CHRIST DIED FOR OUR SINS

The exceeding greatness of God's plan of salvation shows
the perfections of the love of God.

> For all have sinned and fall short of the glory
> of God, and are justified by his grace as a gift,
> through the redemption that is in Christ Jesus,
> whom God put forward as a propitiation by his
> blood, to be received by faith. This was to show
> God's righteousness, because in his divine for-
> bearance he had passed over former sins. It was
> to show his righteousness at the present time,
> so that he might be just and the justifier of the
> one who has faith in Jesus. Romans 3:23-26 ESV.

In this passage, Paul described the *delay* in our sentencing
to a second death of eternal hell as "divine forbearance." Every
person since Adam is like the man living on death row, who is
called a "dead man walking" by his fellow inmates. The condemnation is sure, and he is already called "dead."

Until we put our faith in God through Jesus, we are all the
walking dead. As Paul wrote,

> And you, who were dead in your trespasses
> and the uncircumcision of your flesh, God
> made alive together with him, having forgiven
> us all our trespasses, by canceling the record

**of debt that stood against us with its legal
demands. This he set aside, nailing it to the
cross.** Colossians 2:13-14 ESV.

Paul was saying that this is a *legal issue* worked out for
us in Jesus Christ as our merciful, court appointed defense
counsel. Just as a legal pronouncement of the curse of death
was made on Adam and Eve, God requires a legal process to
bring forgiveness. The more you understand how God did it,
the more you will praise him.

But it is not necessary to become a lawyer to receive
pardon! The quick version is simple and powerful. Paul summarized his gospel this way: **For I delivered unto you first of
all that which I also received, how that Christ died for our
sins according to the scriptures; And that he was buried, and
that he rose again the third day according to the scriptures** (1
Corinthians 15:3-4 KJV).

Before his conversion Paul served under Gamaliel, who
was the equal of our national Attorney General. He himself was
a protege to Gamaliel (Acts 22:3) and perhaps had replaced
Gamaliel by his willingness to persecute the Christians.

Although he knew the Old Testament backwards and for-
wards, yet Paul says he received the gospel message in very
simple terms. Maybe he is here repeating the words of Ananias,
an ordinary, faithful disciple who was sent to him in Damascus
(Acts 9). **Christ died for our sins according to the scriptures.** We also must simply believe in the resurrected Jesus
who is alive today and ask God for forgiveness of our sins.
Jesus said, **This is the work of God, that you believe in him
whom he has sent** (John 6:29 ESV).

The Sufficiency of Christ's Offering

The truth of the gospel of Jesus is that Jesus offered himself
as a sacrifice on our behalf. His death was fully sufficient to end

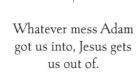

Whatever mess Adam got us into, Jesus gets us out of.

the curse of death physically and spiritually. Paul used an extended dialog to teach how Jesus was an "opposite Adam" on our behalf (Romans 5:12-21). Whatever mess Adam got us into, Jesus gets us out of. That may not be great grammar, but it is powerful knowledge. Whatever Adam lost is restored to us in Jesus Christ as we walk in "unfeigned faith" (1 Timothy 1:5).

One way that Paul taught the sufficiency of the death of Christ to deliver us from the curse of death was to call Jesus's death on the cross "a curse." **Christ redeemed us from the curse of the law by becoming a curse for us--for it is written, "Cursed is everyone who is hanged on a tree"–** (Galatians 3:13 ESV). Paul is quoting Deuteronomy 21:23.

The Romans were brutally efficient at the task of crucifixion. No man ever left a cross alive. They plunged a spear into the side of Jesus after he died to prove his heart had ruptured and all his blood had congealed, confirming he was dead. In his letter to the Galatians Paul taught that Jesus died by human hands, and called the death sentence a "curse," following the language of the Jewish law. Paul did not say Jesus became the curse itself, because he specifically added a comment that being "hanged on the tree" (crucified) is what "cursed" means. The penalty of sin is death, and Jesus died "for our sins." **Therefore, just as sin came into the world through one man, and death through sin, and so death spread to all men because all sinned–** (Romans 5:12 ESV). Jesus was not the curse because being put to death is the curse. When Paul wrote "Jesus became the curse for us" he means "Jesus became dead for us."

In Romans 5:14 Paul wrote that death was a curse that has reigned since Adam, even before any death sentence in Moses's law. Jesus not only had to die to satisfy the Law of Moses, but also to cure the sentence of death put on every person descended from Adam. In dying according to the Law, Jesus became "a curse for us," meaning he died in our place and for our benefit. Remember the definition of curse in a previous discussion where it was explained that "curse" is not evil speaking, but a righteous judgment given to punish sin.

Jesus was in no way personally accursed (i.e., rejected by God) when he died for us. Paul made this clear in writing to the Corinthian church. **Therefore I make known to you that no one speaking by *the* Spirit of God says Jesus *is* a curse, and *that* no one can say that Jesus *is* Lord, but by the Holy Spirit** (1 Corinthians 12:3 MKJV). Paul called the *method of death* a "curse for us" because it was a legal execution that we deserved, not Jesus. "For us" indicates substitution. In as much as Jesus died by being hung on a wooden cross ("a tree"), Paul saw in Deuteronomy a foreshadowing of the death of Jesus "for us." (Note: Peter also used the word "tree" to refer to the cross in 1 Peter 2:24. Apparently it was a common synonym for "cross" among Jewish believers in Christ.)

To call Jesus "accursed," as if He was hated by God, is a misapplication of Paul's meaning. The same bad theology is at work when Jesus is called "actual sin" when quoting 2 Corinthians 5:21. **For our sake he made him to be sin who knew no sin, so that in him we might become the righteousness of God** (2 Corinthians 5:21 ESV). Jesus died as a sacrifice for sin in the place of the sinner, a holy substitute who bore the physical death sentence prescribed by Jewish law for sin. In the Old Testament the simple word "sin" was used for either a sinful act *or* the holy sacrificial animal that died because of the sin of a repentant offeror.

Because sin and the sacrifice for sin are opposites, the context was sufficient to know which was meant. "Sin" is an evil and rebellious act, but a "sin offering" was a naturally unblemished, specified animal that removed the guilt of sin when it died in a manner prescribed in the Law. Technically speaking, the Greek sentence begins with "For him who knew not sin..." so Paul highlighted the sinlessness of Jesus by mentioning that fact first. "The sinless one was made the sin-offering..." is the meaning. This should shock us at the opposition of Christ's sinlessness with our guilt that caused him to suffer death.

In his letter to the Galatian church Paul said this method of death on a cross was "a curse for us" (Galatians 3:13 ESV). "For us" means the benefit is ours because Jesus was paying the price of our sin that was death. Jesus foretold his voluntary death long before it happened when he said, **For this reason the Father loves me, because I lay down my life that I may take it up again** (John 10:17 ESV). Because Jesus never sinned, the death on the cross could not be a curse upon him personally. Rather, he was made "a curse for us" bearing the death we deserved in our place. Therefore, we call the work of Christ a "substitutionary sacrifice."

The sufficiency of the death of Christ to cover all the sins of all who believe in Him is broadly attested in the New Testament. **But if we walk in the light, as he is in the light, we have fellowship with one another, and the blood of Jesus his Son cleanses us from all sin** (1 John 1:7 ESV).

Also, we read, **But when Christ had offered for all time a single sacrifice for sins, he sat down at the right hand of God... For by a single offering, he has perfected for all time those who are being sanctified** (Hebrews 10:12-14 ESV). The death of Jesus was never a "normal and average" death because the redeeming value of this one death broke the curse of death off all who will believe on his name.

I wrote before that Jesus in his suffering on the cross fulfilled the payment of God's penalty of death, removing from us any further prosecution for past offences (Hebrews 2:9 and 10:12). By God's decree, we are therefore set free from our past lives as offenders against God's righteousness. As Paul wrote: **And such were some of you. But you were washed, you were sanctified, you were justified in the name of the Lord Jesus Christ and by the Spirit of our God** (1 Corinthians 6:11 ESV). And, **There is therefore now no condemnation for those who are in Christ Jesus** (Romans 8:1 ESV).

Jesus paid in full our debt for sins committed against God and his creation, thereby cancelling all future legal obligations and prosecutions. In his death there is a full pardon for us. This is something to rejoice about!

THE PHYSICAL DEATH
OF JESUS ON THE CROSS

Why do the New Testament references to the death of Jesus emphasize his physical sufferings and death? It is precisely because God instituted physical death as the judgment for our sin (Genesis 3:19). Physical death and eternal punishment are not alternatives, but physical death is the precursor to eternal damnation. The emphasis on physical death does not diminish the reality of eternal punishment. Both are understood as the judgment due to our sinning against God.

God set an order in the imposition of the full penalty of death. First there was physical death. That death will progress to eternal death unless the sinner is forgiven. Both are horrific consequences for our rebellion; the second worse than the first. God allowed time before physical death for sinners to repent and therefore avoid the eternal punishment that is sure to come if we die unrepentant.

The price of our salvation, the payment for our sins, must be first understood as physical death. God's words of judgment in Genesis chapter 3 included strained relationships, unproductive ground, and death that turned man back to dust. Since then, the universal experience of humanity is one of a physical universe thoroughly locked into death. Although we grasp for all we can get from life, we are never far from death. There is no peace to be found in life because death seems to be having the last laugh at us and is always blocking our way to a lasting happiness and stability.

Death is the great problem for humanity. I recently heard a commentary on Elon Musk and the major cultural influences of his innovative companies. But the commentator noted that his future projects are now coming under scrutiny because of his own limited lifetime. This year he turned 51. People are not questioning his genius but rather his ability to match the major accomplishments of the past due to the limits of his human life span on earth. Most people die with "great plans."

People are casual toward being reconciled to God because they do not sense the danger of his warnings. They are more concerned with the fear of their own deaths. God has designed our lifetimes to sense this death drawing closer with age so that every person will awaken to the need of reconciliation to God. As the people around us die, the reality of physical death around us is the warning shot, the "shot over the bow," to warn us "to flee from the wrath to come" (Matthew 3:7).

God has framed the question "What is the purpose of life?" with the four borders of the undeniability of death. The question of fulfilling purpose in life is cut short on every side as our plans meet with death! Therefore, we cannot answer the question of the purpose of life without bringing up a discussion of death. When someone asks "What is life for?" then futility and frustration cause one to say "Eat, drink, and be happy, for tomorrow we die." Why work 18 hours a day to build a rocket ship to Mars if it will be completed 10 years after your life expectancy? The thinking person (when not dulled to senselessness by partying) must pause from their labors and ponder life, death, and God.

Some people try to ignore death with mind-numbing entertainments. Others plan living trusts, memorials, or foundations that will benefit others after they are "gone." None of these efforts deal directly with death because humanity is powerless to negotiate with it. A few of the super-rich will freeze their brains hoping that the janitor will not accidentally leave the freezer unplugged. For the rest, death is like hitting a brick wall.

Nevertheless, the fear of death keeps the religious quest alive in a secular world. God uses his delay of the enforcement of death to allow sinners to seek him. The reality of death forces the average person to ask questions about God and eternity now in this life before it is too late. The gospel of Jesus Christ is the answer to those questions.

When Jesus came into the world, he took on the flesh and blood "body of this death" (Romans 7:24), but without sin. Since therefore the children share in flesh and blood, **he himself likewise partook of the same things, that through death he might destroy the one who has the power of death, that is, the devil, and deliver all those who through fear of death were subject to lifelong slavery** (Hebrews 2:14-15 ESV). The battle for the redemption of man was fought in the flesh-and-blood body of Jesus Christ against the devil who sought to kill Jesus before his mission was fulfilled.

Scripturally, the plan of God was, and is, to accomplish the eternal redemption of individuals in the world of physical life. The Bible nowhere says we will become angels when we die. The entire idea of "resurrection" is foreign to a transition from flesh to spirit. Jesus came into this world as the "word become flesh" (John 1:14). At the price of his own flesh subjected to the will of his spirit, he offered himself to his Father God. **I am the living bread that came down from heaven. If anyone eats of this bread, he will live forever. And the bread that I will give for the life of the world is my flesh** (John 6:51 ESV).

He that was of heaven (spirit) came into the physical world (flesh) because that is where condemned humanity resides under the sentence of physical death. It was the sight and touch of Jesus as "flesh and bone" that taught the disciples what the Father in heaven was like, and later convinced the disciples that the resurrection was true (Luke 24:39).

Jesus did not come into the world with a goal of pulling Man's spirit out of his body and depositing it in heaven. But that seems to be the way salvation is perceived in many churches. He offered his flesh to death through the eternal Spirit as a redeeming sacrifice. **How much more will the blood of Christ, who through the eternal Spirit offered himself without blemish to God, purify our conscience from dead**

works to serve the living God (Hebrews 9:14 ESV). The eternal Spirit worked through the blood of Jesus Christ.

The reluctance of some theologians to see the arena of conflict in physical terms has led to some weird theories of a "spiritual" redemption. The Scriptures show that flesh and spirit were *united* in the life of Jesus to work out our redemption. The physical sufferings of Jesus included the submission of his flesh to spiritually worthy goals. He became our example in overcoming temptations. **For because he himself has suffered when tempted, he is able to help those who are being tempted** (Hebrews 2:18 ESV).

The life of Jesus that he offered to God on the cross was a unity of flesh, blood, and spirit. The perfection of Jesus is one of body, soul, and spirit; and these three all work together. **...how much more will the blood of Christ, who through the eternal Spirit offered himself without blemish to God, purify our conscience from dead works to serve the living God** (Hebrews 9:14 ESV).

In our innermost hearts, we do not want a spiritual redemption apart from the flesh. We want a full redemption that includes self-mastery of worthless and hurtful desires. Paul thought this way: **Have nothing to do with irreverent, silly myths. Rather train yourself for godliness; for while bodily training is of some value, godliness is of value in every way, as it holds promise for the present life and also for the life to come** (1 Timothy 4:7-8 ESV).

We want victory over weaknesses of the flesh. We crave God's leading in our lives. **For we are his workmanship, created in Christ Jesus for good works, which God prepared beforehand, that we should walk in them** (Ephesians 2:10 ESV). The physical sufferings of Christ match our struggles in the flesh. This strengthens our faith and encourages our hearts. He is our hero.

A true Christian does not want excuses for bad behavior but forgiveness that leads to good works. As we mature, confession of our faults and weaknesses as sins turns into a prayer for righteous behavior in our body and spirit. Prayer for forgiveness is itself a cry for help defeating our unbelief (Mark 9:24).

This is why the death of Jesus in the flesh is intricately bound up with our full redemption. Jesus "laid down his life" for a redemptive purpose. Paul taught that our victory over destructive behaviors was found in a unity with the death of Jesus. **We know that our old self was crucified with him in order that the body of sin might be brought to nothing, so that we would no longer be enslaved to sin** (Romans 6:6 ESV). The physical death of Jesus is vitally important to our redemption now and in eternity.

THE DELAY BEFORE THE ETERNAL DEATH SENTENCE

If we receive God's grace before we die, then we will not "die in our sins" (John 8:24). This phrasing of Jesus about "dying in sin" was a reference to the full curse of death that extends beyond physical death. Jesus was clearly saying that there is a worse fate than death of the body. For an atheist, this is a call to become aware of the continuation of the life that is beyond physical death because God will be the judge of every person's life. To the religious, this is a warning that association with religion is not the same as personal faith in the living God. In John 8 Jesus told them of the necessity to believe that he is the Son of God. They protested to Jesus that they were God's children due to their lineage from Abraham. Jesus said that knowledge of the Scriptures yields no benefit without himself as the key to the Scriptures (John 5:39).

The danger of dying unforgiven is the unavoidable sentencing to the lake of fire at the great white throne judgment that is called in Scripture "the second death" (Revelation 20:6). The warnings of all the prophets of all ages agree on one theme: the necessity to avoid punishment by repenting now in this life while there is the opportunity. Paul wrote that the law of God makes the whole world accountable to God (Romans 3:19), **for all have sinned and fall short of the glory of God** (Romans 3:23 ESV).

———————— ✝ ————————

The fact that we still have time to repent before we die is confirmation that the sentencing to eternal punishment is yet future.

————————————————

The fact that we still have time to repent before we die is confirmation that the sentencing to eternal punishment is yet future. Paul wrote that "all (persons) have sinned" and are in danger of eternal punishment. Even those who later come to trust in Christ were formerly condemned (Romans 3:23,24). Those who have not yet trusted in Christ Jesus remain under the curse of physical death and are "under condemnation" that will lead to eternal hell. This is the danger of "dying in your sins."

But no one is locked into punishment if they receive God's offer of reconciliation. Both the condemned sinner and the demons were, and are now, living in the calm before the storm. Demons are guaranteed a future torment but are still subject to a certain freedom now. All of us who sin have enough freedom to hear God's command to turn away from sinning and believe in His Son before we die.

The demons said to Jesus, **What have you to do with us, O Son of God? Have you come here to torment us before the time?** (Matthew 8:29 ESV). The time for confinement in hell had not yet come, so Jesus allowed them to go into a herd of pigs when they were cast out of the crazed man. Demons know their inescapable judgment is approaching, but most people live in ignorance that eternal punishment is avoidable.

The delay in the enforcement of the death sentence should be used as an opportunity for repentance and faith in Jesus. Redemption through Christ can cancel our appointment with hell. John the baptizer admonished his hearers, **Who warned you to flee from the wrath to come?** (Luke 3:7 ESV). This was a stern word of condemnation but not a hopeless abandonment to the future hell. John said that they could prove their repentance by bearing the fruit of repentance (Matthew 3:5-12), and by putting their faith in the coming Savior.

THE TWO DEATHS DISTINCTION

The subject of death is not simple. The context of the word "death" will show what kind of death is being referred to. The death sentence given to Adam when he sinned determined that he would return to the dust of the ground at the end of his life. This is physical death. God purposefully made the distinction of physical death (a first death) and a "second death" (Revelation 2:11). God made the distinction and gave us his fuller revelation of what death is.

In Genesis 3 God pronounced that Adam's sin would be punished with a "dust to dust" sentence of physical death. Adam stood as the representative of all his descendants, and death spread into the world. Adam stood at the beginning of humanity. This truth was important to Paul. **For as in Adam all die, so also in Christ shall all be made alive** (1 Corinthians 15:22 ESV). God separated the sentencing of the first death from the second future sentencing when He made no reference to a second death when He first pronounced judgment on Adam.

From the day of the first sin, God set a time for final judgment at the end of the age, after all people lived, so that every life would be judged on its own merits, not just the sin of Adam. He set a judgment day hearing as a future "court date" that can be compared to a sentencing hearing. **Then I saw a great white throne and him who was seated on it... And the dead were judged by what was written in the books, according to what they had done** (Revelation 20:11-12 ESV).

Note that a sentencing hearing is a judicial event held *after conviction*. It determines the kind and extent of the punishment that is appropriate for the prior conviction. God is not bound by the variations of judicial procedures of any nation, but there are general parallels. Physical death is currently in effect as the sentencing given to Adam, and we are all included in it. Paul wrote, "in Adam all die" (1 Corinthians 15:22 and see Romans 5:12).

The first and second deaths are roughly equivalent to one's physical life on earth and the after-death eternal state. The judgment of death on Adam covers both. God has blended us into a composite creature of flesh and spirit made in His own image. Nevertheless, God Himself has distinguished between the death of the body and eternal death by describing the lake of fire that appears after the millennial reign of Jesus as the "second death" (Revelation 20:14).

The term "second death" is a term of prominence, used four times in the apostle John's book, Revelation. When Paul wrote the words, **In Adam all die...** he was referring to the first kind of death which is physical. This is the kind of death that is currently in effect. All humanity stands convicted and condemned to the second death in our natural state, but it is not imposed until the great white throne judgment. God offers an escape from the second death through personal repentance and faith in Jesus before we die.

The two deaths distinction has a direct impact on the theology of the atonement. Looking at the whole of Scripture, the judgment for Adam's sin was dying in two ways: a physical death ("dust to dust") and an eternal punishment from God (Revelation 20:10,14-15). The sentencing currently in effect is the physical death that God pronounced in Genesis 3. God decided that there will be no sentencing to eternal punishment until the time when Jesus will judge all the works of mankind at one great judgment event at the end of the age. At that event, Jesus's own perfect life in the flesh will be the condemnation of all human sin, even as his holiness has qualified him as judge of the world (Revelation 5:3-5).

Both deaths are the result of one conviction. Adam was directly warned not to disobey, or he would experience death. **...but of the tree of the knowledge of good and evil you shall not eat, for in the day that you eat of it you shall surely die** (Genesis

2:17 ESV). But Adam did sin and all his descendants have been guilty of rebellion since Adam's sin. Each of his descendants has added his own sin to Adam's sinning. All are guilty (convicted) before God, and currently condemned (John 3:18,36).

The gap between the sentencing to physical death in Genesis 3 and the judgment at the end of the age is deliberate on God's part. This delay allows every person already guilty and under sentence of death to live their own lifetime, having time to repent and be forgiven. That is what God wants. **The Lord is not slow to fulfill his promise as some count slowness, but is patient toward you, not wishing that any should perish, but that all should reach repentance** (2 Peter 3:9 ESV). If a person refuses to repent, then they are without excuse before God. A final judgment at the end of earth's history will be based upon individual deeds, so that no one may argue that it was unjust to inherent Adam's curse (Revelation 20:12).

Jesus died physically to redeem all who repent and submit to the Lordship of Christ. In doing so he legally stayed the process of future punishment to eternal damnation for those who believe in him. **Blessed and holy is the one who shares in the first resurrection! Over such the second death has no power, but they will be priests of God and of Christ, and they will reign with him for a thousand years** (Revelation 20:6 ESV).

Physical death was the mission focus of the incarnation at the first coming of Jesus. Jesus taught us, **I did not come to judge the world but to save the world** (John 12:47 ESV). But he also taught us that he is coming again. **When the Son of Man comes in his glory, and all the angels with him, then he will sit on his glorious throne** (Matthew 25:31-46 ESV).

The focus of the second coming of Christ is his judgment of the whole world as King of Kings. Peter preached, **And he commanded us to preach to the people and to testify that he is the one appointed by God to be judge of the living and the dead** (Acts 10:42 ESV). His first coming focused on the first death, and his second coming will deal with the second death.

Not only did Jesus in his humanity prove that God could be perfectly obeyed by a flesh and blood person, but also his perfect life qualified him as the substitute in death for sinners. **Since therefore the children share in flesh and blood, he himself likewise partook of the same things, that through death he might destroy the one who has the power of death, that is, the devil** (Hebrews 2:14 ESV). In the first coming Jesus died in the flesh to redeem us from the curse of physical death.

THE REALITY OF ETERNAL DEATH

The patience of Jesus was severely tested as he lived in a world of sinners. They caused him a lot of grief. Once when the disciples could not cast out a demon, he said, **O faithless and twisted generation, how long am I to be with you? How long am I to bear with you? Bring him here to me.** (Matthew 17:17 ESV). Clearly, he had high expectations for his disciples. His usual demeanor was that of a servant rather than a task master. He was the opposite of so many employers and government officials today who seem to enjoy making people under their control squirm and feel the pressure.

Most of the time when Jesus ran into ignorance or unbelief, Jesus just kept on teaching. When he mentioned the reality of eternal punishment it was not with any pride or desire to show dominance. His warnings were sincere. Eternal punishment was a real punishment, and a true danger.

The reality of eternal punishment is based upon the teaching of Jesus. It came forth in the context of "causing the little ones who believe in me to stumble" (Mark 9:42). But true to character Jesus did not let his disciples rest at the thought of others bearing harsh punishments like being thrown in the sea with a millstone tied around their neck. His next words were directly aimed at them.

Jesus told them, **And if your hand causes you to sin, cut it off. It is better for you to enter life crippled than with two hands to go to hell, to the unquenchable fire** (Mark 9:43 ESV). In eternal hell there is fire that will never go out. Choosing the words of Isaiah, Jesus quoted the closing words of Isaiah's book, **for their worm shall not die, neither shall their fire be quenched** (Isaiah 66:24 KJV). Jesus was not breaking new prophetic ground here but was confirming the words of Isaiah.

In the same passage Isaiah mentioned a new heavens and a new earth. The Revelation of John recorded that the appearance of the new heavens and a new earth was immediately preceded by populating the eternal lake of fire with those condemned in the final judgment. This is called the second death.

There is a judgment to be feared that surpasses the tragedy of losing a critical body part. The undying worm and the unquenchable fire are words describing a torment of unsurpassable agonies to be avoided at all costs.

Deliverance from Eternal Death

The sentence of God on Adam was specifically stated as physical death, as we already have discussed. This is why Jesus had to suffer by the shedding of his life's blood unto death on the cross. The substitution of the life of the Son of God for our lives is at the core of the meaning of Paul's words, **Christ died for our sins in accordance with the Scriptures** (1 Corinthians 15:3).

As we might expect, the Christian doctrine of the atonement of Christ is about as complex as it could be. In the theology of the atonement are the forgiveness of sins, the validation of the holiness of God, the gift of eternal life, the reconciliation of Man and God, the imputation of righteousness to the sinner, the miracles of Jesus, the impartation of the Spirit of God to mankind and the unification of Christ and His people like a bride and a bridegroom for eternity. The biblical doctrine of redemption must account for deliverance from punishment for sins both in this world and beyond death. Only then can it be a full salvation.

How was the death of Jesus on the cross a sufficient sacrifice to cover the sinner's liability for eternal death? Should there be a division of the physical and spiritual dimensions? How do we bridge the temporal and the eternal? We should not dwell on the differences of the earthly and heavenly realms, as if they are not connected. In fact, we find that they are melded perfectly into one in the person of Messiah Jesus, the eternal Word of God who became flesh and lived among us (John 1:14).

> **He is the image of the invisible God, the first-born of all creation. For by him all things were created, in heaven and on earth, visible and invisible, whether thrones or dominions or rulers or authorities--all things were created through him and for him. And he is before all things, and in him all things hold together. And he is the head of the body, the church. He is the beginning, the firstborn from the dead, that in everything he might be preeminent. For in him all the fullness of God was pleased to dwell, and through him to reconcile to himself all things, whether on earth or in heaven, making peace by the blood of his cross.** Colossians 1:15-20 ESV.

Many preachers have viewed the death of Christ wrongly. They have determined, without guidance from apostolic preaching, that the punishment for sins must be accomplished "spiritually" and not physically. Such a line of thought trivializes the sufferings of Jesus and his death by crucifixion. The idea of "substitution" became overwhelming in their interpretation of the death of Christ. They reasoned, "Our sins deserve eternal hell, so eternal hell is what Jesus experienced on the cross instead of us."

They do not mean the cross was a hell of an experience. They say Jesus suffered a spiritual rejection of God that was the equivalent of hell itself, and totally separate from his physical sufferings and death. Following this line of reasoning they teach that "Jesus went to hell for us." There are more worms in this can than can be sorted out here, but I will touch on the subject.

Must the idea of substitution be read into every biblical interpretation of the atonement? Did Jesus suffer hell (the second death) or its equivalent in his spirit as our substitute? If Jesus died to pay our debt of sin only, then is Man only restored to the natural life Adam had before he sinned? How do we receive the gift of eternal life by substitution? How can a (supposed) separation of Jesus from the Father for 3 hours during the crucifixion be the substitution for an eternity in hell? What is the relationship of the death of Jesus on the cross to our deliverance from eternal death at the last great judgment?

The cross of Christ is the center axis of God's work in the world to maintain his justice with respect to the rebellion of sin, and to fulfill his loving plan of sharing His own life by giving humanity the gift of life. Certainly, the complexities of the physical world and the mysteries of the spiritual world both meet at the cross in the person of Jesus Christ.

We must reasonably ask, "Did Jesus on the cross have to suffer the torments of eternal hell if hell had not yet been implemented as a judgment?" The answer is, No. Jesus only suffered in our place for the punishment pronounced upon us in Genesis 3, which is physical death.

There is no sentencing to eternal hell until the future great white throne judgment. To some ears, this is almost blasphemy. But let's walk through this theology step by step so that the reader

————————+————————

Jesus did not go to hell for us. He died to keep us from being placed in hell.

————————————————

may appreciate what Jesus has done for us! Jesus did not go to hell for us. He died to keep us from being placed in hell.

When Jesus died for us, he reconciled us to God for our guilt of sins committed in this life. Also, the legal sentencing of physical death (Genesis 3) was satisfied in the physical death of Christ as our substitute. This is biblical and apostolic. **And you, who once were alienated and hostile in mind, doing evil deeds, he has now reconciled in his body of flesh by his death, in order to present you holy and blameless and above reproach before him** (Colossians 1:21-22 ESV). Paul wrote that through Adam's sin death reigned in all men. Jesus died "in his body of flesh" for our sins to release us from the curse of death that was the punishment for our sins and to give us a new holy and blameless nature.

Jesus fulfilled the demand of God's justice on our behalf that a sinner must die for his sin. *Forgiveness of sins cancels any future punishments because God ceases the prosecution against us.* Jesus did not have to suffer the "potential" punishments of repentant sinners, only the physical death that was already prescribed and required in Adam's sentencing (Genesis 3:19).

Paul wrote that God nailed the charges against us to the cross (Colossians 2:14). The charges were the legal demands of God against sinners, the chief of which was the curse of death given in Genesis 3. The word "charges" has been translated as "ordinances" (KJV) and "debts" (ESV). Paul says these legal debts were "nailed to the cross," using a figure of speech to signify that they are cancelled.

There was no paper nailed to the cross, only the flesh of Jesus Christ. Because our charges are "crucified," the believer has no more debt of death. We may say that Jesus was killed to satisfy that legal debt. We may also say that because the debt was the death of the sinner that Jesus died as a sinless substitute for the sinner, discharging the debt. The satisfaction of the debt by the death of Christ was the death of the debt. Jesus died and the debt died.

Paul wrote about how Jesus died to satisfy the death that the law required for sinners. He did not mention eternal hell. All sinners are guilty and deserving of hell, but it was not yet a true debt until the sentencing at the final great white throne.

Forgiveness given and applied to sinners before physical death changes everything. There was no need for Jesus to suffer the torments of hell for sinners in a payment-in-kind transaction because the *current* debt to the ordinances of God was paid in full by his physical death.

The "ordinances" and "debts" are now dead (done away with) being nailed to the cross. The prosecution of sins was ended at that point in time when Jesus died for our sins. The case against repentant sinners (i.e., all of us who believe in Jesus) has no continuance to the great white throne judgment, so that they will never be sentenced to eternal hell.

Jesus said that those who are saved "do not come into judgment" (John 5:24). Those who are "saved" will never come into the future judgment where eternal hell is assigned to sinners who "die in their sins" (John 8:24). Therefore, repentant sinners did not require a substitute to suffer a punishment they did not yet owe. No "substitution" is required because a sinner is not assigned to eternal hell until the final judgment. To be sure, they are under the condemnation for sin and are guilty. They would have owed it if they died unforgiven and came into judgment.

But the sentencing event is still future. Therefore, forgiveness ended the prosecution at the point of satisfaction of the legal debt owed *thus far* which was physical death (Genesis 3:19).

When we are born again, the prosecution of our sins is ended! Jesus was explicit on this point. **Truly, truly, I say to you, whoever hears my word and believes him who sent me has eternal life. He does not come into judgment, but has passed from death to life** (John 5:24 ESV). The prosecution of our sins is OVER when we put our faith in Jesus because we have given up our right to be judged individually and we have joined in the "class action" atonement of Jesus Christ.

If a felon dies after his conviction at trial, but before sentencing, do they sentence his dead body to 10 to 20 years in prison? No, the prosecution is terminated. His death has cancelled continuation of the case. Even if someone came forward and said, "Out of love I will serve time for this man's condemnation," the judge would reply, "There is no need, since the case was cancelled, we never had a sentencing." **There is therefore now no condemnation for those who are in Christ Jesus** (Romans 8:1 ESV). We are like the felon who died convicted and guilty, but before sentencing. He was never assigned further punishment after his death, even though he deserved it before his death. Being in Christ, we have no condemnation as of "now." Jesus died for us by satisfying the judgment of physical death imposed on Adam in Genesis 3, and in so doing he cancelled for us a future and otherwise unavoidable sentencing to eternal hell.

> **And you, who were dead in your trespasses and the uncircumcision of your flesh, God made alive together with him, having forgiven us all our trespasses, by canceling the record of debt that stood against us with its legal demands. This he set aside, nailing it to the cross.** Colossians 2:13-14 ESV.

Remember that in the Bible death came as a judgment on sin: **sin came into the world through one man, and death through sin** (Romans 5:12 ESV). If death is seen only as "natural," then the significance of Jesus dying cannot be understood. The crucifixion must be understood with the biblical understanding of death as the punishment of sin.

Paul taught the subject of death in the light of Old Testament revelation that sinners earned death as wages for their sin. **Therefore, just as sin came into the world through one man, and death through sin, and so death spread to all**

men because all sinned (Romans 5:12 ESV). Many have looked for another basis of atonement by supposing that Jesus had to die a spiritual death to redeem us because they are not looking at sin as the cause of death. Instead, they are only looking at separation from God as the punishment of sin. Therefore, they re-interpret the crucifixion as a time of spiritual isolation from God, instead of the fulfilment of the judgment of God that sin will bring death (Genesis 2:17). These commentators have not understood what Paul taught: **For the wages of sin is death, but the free gift of God is eternal life in Christ Jesus our Lord** (Romans 6:23 ESV).

Jesus died and we died in him because he said, **Greater love has no one than this, that someone lay down his life for his friends** (John 15:13 ESV). Those who are forgiven in Jesus are not going to eternal hell because Jesus stopped the prosecution with his bodily death, all at his expense. Paul says we were made alive together with him. You are free to go!

WHY DO WE STILL DIE?

If Jesus died in substitution for our death penalty, then why do we still die physically? Hasn't the curse of death been destroyed? We do still all die, but Paul wrote that we are not hopeless because the resurrection of Jesus showed us that our future reversal of death is assured. **But we do not want you to be uninformed, brothers, about those who are asleep, that you may not grieve as others do who have no hope** (1 Thessalonians 4:13 ESV).

There is so much we do not yet understand. Even though God is eternal, He has chosen to work within time, with beginnings and endings, with covenants, with individuals, and nations. It is too complicated for a flow chart. I believe the answer as to why we still experience death of the body has several potential answers.

One answer is to see that although God made promises to us as individuals He also is working with the world as a whole system. Adam's sin brought a punishment of death shared by his descendants and the earth also (Genesis 3:17). God worked to bring individuals to repentance and faith one person at a time, not having to wait for the redemption of the earth. Jesus taught that the gift of eternal life is given at the point of faith to us individually (John 5:24), and that the redemption of the body will come at the end of the age when all creation will be released from the curse of death (1Corinthians 15:22).

After the resurrection of Jesus, the disciples thought that surely the time had come for Israel to be restored as queen of the nations of the earth. Jesus told them "No" because there were times and seasons of God's will (Acts 1:6-7). Physical death is a fixed part of this world order and the sentencing of "dust to dust" endures for now in the world order. God gives us the gift of eternal life when we believe in Jesus, so that death of the body becomes bearable.

Jesus said that the kingdom of God is within us (Luke 17:21), but also we are to pray for it to come over all the earth (Matthew 6:10). Like the kingdom, the resurrections will follow an order and timing set by God. **For as in Adam all die, even so in Christ shall all be made alive. But every man in his own order: Christ the firstfruits; afterward they that are Christ's at his coming** (1 Corinthians 15:22-23 KJV). Paul said that death is the ultimate enemy and is determined for total defeat at the proper time. **For he must reign until he has put all his enemies under his feet. The last enemy to be destroyed is death** (1 Corinthians 15:25-26 ESV).

God takes the sting of death out of dying when we believe our way through it in hope of the resurrection of the righteous. Jesus said, **Truly, truly, I say to you, whoever hears my word and believes him who sent me has eternal life. He does not come into judgment, but has passed from death to life** (John 5:24 ESV). He counteracts the pain and loss of physically dying with hope and faith in the restoration of all things. For example, if a person believes in Jesus while in jail for a crime, there may be some time remaining to serve in prison. Even though God has forgiven him, the State has not. God gives that person strength to endure and leads him to make best use of the time.

We know from the testimony of many persons that their attitude toward death was completely transformed after their re-birth by faith in Jesus. Our attitude changes because we understand God rules over history. He gives us the gift of eternal life as soon as we are born again, and therefore death is no longer a punishment but becomes a passage. Although we die, we do not die "in our sins" to face eternal punishment.

When Jesus went to Bethany to raise Lazarus from the dead, Martha thought it was too late for him to be healed. Nevertheless, she confessed her faith that her brother would participate in the resurrection of the righteous at the end of the age. We are not different from Martha and her faith. Jesus said to Martha, **I am the resurrection and the life. Whoever believes in me, though he die, yet shall he live, and everyone who lives and believes in me shall never die. Do you believe this?** (John 11:25-26 ESV).

Jesus was not in Bethany to hurt the feelings of those he loved. He was there to comfort them with his truth. In this passage we see that he was teaching a truth about a believer's attitude toward death, and the believer's experience of death. Our attitude is that if we die, our resurrection is assured. Spiritually speaking, we have already received the gift of eternal life. We know what Jesus said is true: **everyone who lives and believes in me shall never die**. Dying is no longer experienced as a punishment, but just another day in the eternal life God has gifted us in Christ.

This was an appropriate time to teach this truth because Jesus was raising Lazarus up and restoring his physical life. This teaching would help him face dying the next time with confidence in the plan of God. Can you imagine what went through Lazarus's heart and mind as he approached dying the second time? How could he not be filled with hopeful expectations?

Thank God that John recorded this account for the encouragement of all of us.

The assurance of the Spirit of God in us comforts us and carries us through all difficulties and even the death of the body until the time when resurrection is planned for all the righteous at one time. For more discussion of this topic, go to the sections "Believers in Jesus Do Not Come Under Judgment" and "Ending the Fear of Death."

ONE ATONEMENT IN TIME FOR ALL TIME

The atonement of Jesus Christ is a wonder of God's planning and a wonder of the love of Jesus in laying down his life to reconcile the ungodly to God. All the Lord Jesus really asks of us is our willingness to believe what he has done, and to get on track in his training in righteousness. He said, **Take my yoke upon you, and learn from me, for I am gentle and lowly in heart, and you will find rest for your souls. For my yoke is easy, and my burden is light** (Matthew 11:29-30 ESV).

Because the pre-existent Son of God took on flesh to live as the Son of Man (a true human being), Jesus was able to live a perfect life on earth so that he could then offer his life to God for the satisfaction of the judgment of death on our behalf. Jesus said he laid down his life for the "sheep of his pasture," who are those who believe him.

In the simplest words I can write, here is a summary: We rebelled against God with our sins. God sentenced us to die. Jesus volunteered to be executed instead of us. By our repentance and faith, he cleared all our past liabilities, gave us a new nature, eternal life, and full inheritance rights as children of God in his eternal kingdom. Physical death is no longer a punishment, but a passage into the presence of the Lord Jesus. Our life, from the first day of faith in Jesus, is living personally under his Lordship, and we are personally filled with God's Holy Spirit, awaiting the return of Jesus to earth, our resurrection, and citizenship in God's eternal kingdom.

Do not become confused with physical time. The death of Jesus happened within earth-time where we live, and it only needed to happen once. God made new life available to all believers by faith in Jesus as the Savior of the world.

> **Long ago, at many times and in many ways, God spoke to our fathers by the prophets, but in these last days he has spoken to us by his Son, whom he appointed the heir of all things, through whom also he created the world. He is the radiance of the glory of God and the exact imprint of his nature, and he upholds the universe by the word of his power. After making purification for sins, he sat down at the right hand of the Majesty on high, having become as much superior to angels as the name he has inherited is more excellent than theirs.**
> Hebrews 1:1-4 ESV.

Jesus was only required to give up his life on the cross once to affect such a great salvation for faithful believers of all time. The Old Testament sacrifices were forward-looking types and prophetic shadows of the sacrifice of Christ. Individuals who offered a sacrifice or offering before Jesus was born were acting in good faith to offer what God prescribed at that time for forgiveness. God honored their faith and tied it to the cross of Jesus in the future. **We have been sanctified through the offering of the body of Jesus Christ once for all** (Hebrews 10:10 ESV).

Those who hear the gospel of Jesus must exercise faith in him to be saved. As Peter preached to Cornelius, **To him all the prophets bear witness that everyone who believes in him receives forgiveness of sins through his name** (Acts 10:43 ESV). Paul wrote that Abraham was saved by his faith, and we are likewise saved by faith (Romans 4:16). Today we trust in the revealed personal name of God which is "Jesus," but saving faith has always been in the one true God. Jesus is the way to God as our Father (John 14:6; 17:3).

The death of Jesus was effective for our salvation because he died for us in the flesh. When he physically laid down his life he cried out from the cross, "It is finished." What was finished? His human life was over on earth so that the legal payment of death owed for the judgment on Adam, and the payment for our personal sins, was finished.

Every one of us has confirmed our lineage to the first sinner through our own sinful deeds. Therefore, death is the common lot of all mankind. **Yet death reigned from Adam to Moses, even over those whose sinning was not like the transgression of Adam** (Romans 5:14 ESV). The main issue is not the type of sin we committed, but the disobedience to God that is rebellion. The one atonement in time for all time was Jesus Christ when he shed his life's blood to death for us as the price of reconciliation with God. All believers in God are united in this one self-giving sacrifice of the Son of God for their forgiveness and salvation from the wrath to come.

All believers in God are united in this one self-giving sacrifice of the Son of God for their forgiveness and salvation from the wrath to come.

REDEMPTION BY THE DEATH OF JESUS ON THE CROSS

Let's look at the cross where Jesus died more closely. Jesus by his physical suffering and death paid the penalty of the physical death that sinners deserved. By paying our debt he cancelled the prosecution of our sins that would have sent us to eternal punishment. We have not appreciated the exculpatory power of his death as we should.

All persons who have lived have been guilty of their sins and under the curse of death as they lived out their lives. Without Christ's substitutionary sacrifice there was no hope of forgiveness. Our past life was slavery to the sin we loved. Paul wrote, **The wages of sin is death...** (Romans 6:23 ESV).

But in the Bible God reveals that the death of Jesus was exactly what the Father required for Him to forgive us. The more we study the death of Jesus, the more we see that this death was somehow very different from our own; not in its reality as a real death, but in its merit.

Although most people hate the thought of dying, they accept that death is all around us and is so much a part of creation that it is accepted as normal. Many ask, "How was the death of Jesus any different from the experience of all others?" They do not understand how it had any special merit since every person must die. They assume Jesus ran out of time and was killed for being anti-establishment like Socrates. They do not understand how the life of Jesus had redeeming value, other than as an inspirational story.

This reveals an ignorance of God and how much the severity of sin is underestimated. Human culture normalizes sin and normalizes death, not admitting that death is the result of sin. Christians who teach "the wages of sin is death" are not popular. I am not suggesting that at the next family funeral you openly say, "Well, another sinner bites the dust!" However, there is some truth in it.

When Jesus died in his flesh and blood body, he died the flesh and blood death God required of Adam when he was judged. When Jesus died for us, he broke the power of the curse of death by using his own death to satisfy the sentence of death given to Adam. Each one of us has repeated Adam's error. But Jesus paid for our sin with his death. He stood in our place. Paul wrote, **God shows his love for us in that while we were still sinners, Christ died for us** (Romans 5:8 ESV).

This is the biblical doctrine of substitution.

By personal repentance and faith in Jesus, a sinner takes hold of the virtue of Jesus like a drowning man clings to a life preserver. The Son of God laid down his life at his death as the substitute for sinners, satisfying the penalty of the curse of death pronounced on Adam and inherited by us from Adam. This is the reason why Jesus had to come in a flesh and blood body. This is the key idea in Hebrews 10:4-10.

For God to save us He first had to love us while we were lost in our sins.

> **For one will scarcely die for a righteous person--though perhaps for a good person one would dare even to die-- but God shows his love for us in that while we were still sinners, Christ died for us. Since, therefore, we have now been justified by his blood, much more shall we be saved by him from the wrath of God. For if while we were enemies we were reconciled to God by the death of his Son, much more, now that we are reconciled, shall we be saved by his life.** (Romans 5:7-10 ESV).

This is grace. The only way God could show his love for us was if God did not immediately finalize the sentence of death he placed on Adam. This is the gospel Paul preached. Paul believed the saving grace of God was effectual for us because Christ "died for us while we were sinners." His shed blood was his physical life, and it justified us before God. The "death of his Son" was the method God used to reconcile us to God in this world.

Paul clearly had a two-part redemption in mind when he penned these words. **We have now been justified by his blood, much more shall we be saved by him from the wrath of God.** These two parts are the curse of physical death, and the judgment of the second death. The physical death of Jesus ended the prosecution of our sins, and being justified we will not face the second death.

These verses show that Paul could not express it more clearly, and there was no "spiritualizing" here. Paul was talking about a messy and gruesome death on the cross. This is where our faith in Jesus abides, not in a mystical and spiritualized redemption, but in a literal death that affects us spiritually. We are now justified before God, and therefore we are exempted from a sentencing to hell which is future. We are justified and will be saved when wrath comes at the final judgment on all humanity.

Forgiveness of sins includes the inner gift of God of a new nature purchased by Jesus by a sacrificial and substitutionary physical death. **And you, who once were alienated and hostile in mind, doing evil deeds, he has now reconciled in his body of flesh by his death, in order to present you holy and blameless and above reproach before him...** (Colossians 1:21-22 ESV) This is the apostolic doctrine. Reconciliation with God is based upon "**his body of flesh by his death.**" I will go into this truth in more detail in my next book. Now that you are aware of the importance of the bodily death of Jesus, you will find many references to it in the New Testament, and your faith in what God has done will grow.

I also mentioned a delay. God did not kill Adam the day he sinned. Nevertheless, the process of death began. Christ could only die "while we were yet sinners" if the judgment of death was somehow delayed in a way that was consistent with God's justice. We know from Scripture that God delayed imposing the sentence of physical death on Adam until his days on earth were fulfilled. God built a delay into Adam's death sentence that applies to all of us. It is our physical lifetime.

We all have the opportunity to live out our lives and are spared instantaneous lightning bolts of wrath when we sin. Because God separated the first and second deaths, He has built into every person's life an opportunity to repent before death.

If someone dies unrepentant, he will be raised in a resurrection life to face the great white throne judgment where the sentencing to eternal hell must be completed. But the delay was there while he lived. Without a drawn-out process of the implementation of the curse of death, the end of the world would have been the same day Adam, Eve and the Tempter were all judged guilty.

THE CURSE IS BROKEN WITH FORGIVENESS

Having secured our reconciliation with God by laying down his own life for the death we deserved, Jesus opened the way to the fullness of eternal life for all who believed him. The tragedy at the cross is transformed by the power of its positive accomplishments in our lives. This is how Paul was able to preach about the crucified Messiah with joyful expectation that God would be glorified. The gift of eternal life is accompanied by exemption from the second death, and the proof was the resurrection of Jesus.

When do we get exemption? The moment we believe in Jesus and our sins are forgiven. **Truly, truly, I say to you, whoever hears my word and believes him who sent me has eternal life. He does not come into judgment, but has passed from death to life** (John 5:24 ESV).

Jesus plainly taught that the one who believes in him "**does not come into judgment.**" *The curse that required the death of a sinner is broken when we are forgiven, and further prosecution is cancelled, because Jesus died for our sins.* **Since, therefore, we have now been justified by his blood, much more shall we be saved by him from the wrath of God** (Romans 5:9 ESV).

This "wrath" in the New Testament refers to Jesus coming back to earth to judge the living and the dead at the great white throne judgment. When Peter preached to Cornelius after the resurrection it was still a future judgment. When Paul was writing to the church at Rome, he said it was still a future salvation from wrath. That wrath is eternal punishment in the lake of fire that is called "the second death." When John wrote the Revelation, he prophesied, **Blessed and holy is the one who shares in the first resurrection! Over such the second death has no power, but they will be priests of God and of Christ, and they will reign with him for a thousand years** (Revelation 20:6 ESV).

Jesus, Peter, Paul, and John all agreed that the wrath of God is the future judgment of the whole world in the last days. And they all testified that believers in Jesus will be exempted because they are forgiven. How are they forgiven? Jesus suffered as a substitutionary sacrifice to satisfy the legal penalty of the death sentence given to Adam.

Forgiveness of past sins is granted to those who repent and believe in Jesus. At the moment of new birth in our spirit by the working of the Holy Spirit, further prosecution of eternal hell was cancelled for believers. By faith in Jesus the new believer is tied into the historical death of Jesus who died the death sinners earned for their sins. From that moment the believer is united to Jesus Christ, in covenant with God, and therefore not subject to the wrath of God. He died so that we would not be condemned to hell when he returned as the judge of the whole earth.

All the Scriptures teach this truth. Here are four truths that explain the immediate effects on a person under conviction of sin who cries out to God for forgiveness, believing in the Son of God who suffered the death they deserved.

1. Eternal life is given as God's gift. Forgiveness of personal sins reconciles a person to God and imparts the gift of eternal life at the same moment. **Truly, truly, I say to you, whoever hears my word and believes him who sent me has eternal life. He does not come into judgment but has passed from death to life** (John 5:24 ESV).Eternal life does not begin when we die, or at the return of Jesus, or even

at our resurrection, but is the precious possession of every person who trusts in Jesus for salvation when they believe in him as Messiah, the Son of God.

2. Condemnation of the second death for past sins is removed. There is NOW no condemnation for believers in Christ. A forgiven believer will not be judged and sent to hell for past sins (the second death). **There is therefore now no condemnation for those who are in Christ Jesus. For the law of the Spirit of life has set you free in Christ Jesus from the law of sin and death** (Romans 8:1-2 ESV). The curse of God on sin made us the walking dead because the conviction was certain "in Adam." Without forgiveness in this life, death meant eternal hell was assured. Faith in Jesus means we believe he paid the penalty of death for us, freeing us from the curse. At the moment we believe, our future destiny of the second death is CANCELLED, and we have eternal life as God's gift.

3. A personal relationship with God begins that will continue forever. Every believer is spiritually united to Jesus Christ as Lord as the result of faith in Jesus as Savior. **Therefore, if anyone is in Christ, he is a new creation. The old has passed away; behold, the new has come. All this is from God, who through Christ reconciled us to himself...** (2 Corinthians 5:17-18 ESV).

4. Our adoption as children of God occurs. **But to all who did receive him, who believed in his name, he gave the right to become children of God, who were born, not of blood nor of the will of the flesh nor of the will of man, but of God** (John 1:12-13 ESV).

This is what the cross of Jesus means for all who believe in him. These four truths are integrated and comprise the one truth of "becoming a Christian."

OTHER SCRIPTURES ABOUT FORGIVENESS

Whoever believes in him is not condemned, but whoever does not believe is condemned already, because he has not believed in the name of the only Son of God (John 3:18 ESV).

Christ redeemed us from the curse of the law by becoming a curse for us--for it is written, "Cursed is everyone who is hanged on a tree"-- so that in Christ Jesus the blessing of Abraham might come to the Gentiles, so that we might receive the promised Spirit through faith (Galatians 3:13-14 ESV).

Therefore, if anyone is in Christ, he is a new creation. The old has passed away; behold, the new has come (2 Corinthians 5:17 ESV).

For if while we were enemies we were reconciled to God by the death of his Son, much more, now that we are reconciled, shall we be saved by his life (Romans 5:10 ESV).

For the love of Christ controls us, because we have concluded this: that one has died for all, therefore all have died; and he died for all, that those who live might no longer live for themselves but for him who for their sake died and was raised (2 Corinthians 5:14-15 ESV).

In him you also, when you heard the word of truth, the gospel of your salvation, and believed in him, were sealed with the promised Holy Spirit, who is the guarantee of our inheritance until we acquire possession of it, to the praise of his glory (Ephesians 1:13-14 ESV).

AN ALTERNATIVE TO DEATH

The grace of God provides an alternative to death. People want an answer to the difficulties of life, and God has it. God's redemption includes forgiveness of past sins and a restoration to the path of the maturing process originally planned for Adam. This will be true life, replacing the life we had while under the condemnation of death. The process is progressive maturity in those who believe in Jesus, so that men and women will grow into Christlikeness, as Adam and Eve were supposed to do at the first.

The process can only begin with the spiritual "re-birth" Jesus talked about in John 3. This is God's alternative to death. His life is not given to us like a trophy that sits on a shelf. It is his life-force expressed within us every day. Jesus called the new birth "eternal life" (John 5:24).

The access to the tree of life that was blocked after Adam's sin will come back at the end of the age (Revelation 22:2). Note that the tree of life reappears only after the last great judgment on the sins of mankind in the new Jerusalem. This is the symmetry of the curse of death in history from its first entrance to its last mention.

Adam's judgment brought the first death and blocked access to the tree of life. After the completion of the last judgment, the second death will become the death of death. **Then Death and Hades were thrown into the lake of fire. This is the second death, the lake of fire** (Revelation 20:14 ESV). Immediately, the new Jerusalem will appear wherein "death shall be no more," and the tree of life will be freely available in the middle of the city where its fruits are constantly available.

What a revelation it will be when the tree of life is once again visible and available after restricted access during the history of mankind. The last judgment will be the end of the problem of sin that was an age-long detour in God's original plan for fellowship with Adam and Eve. The tree of life will be the opposite of eternal punishment. God will reside with his people, and it will be eternal life for them.

God's remedy for death is Jesus Christ. Jesus said**, I am the door. If anyone enters by me, he will be saved and will go in and out and find pasture. The thief comes only to steal and**

kill and destroy. I came that they may have life and have it abundantly (John 10:9-10 ESV).

One could describe the mission of Jesus as the end of death. The destruction of death will be the removal of the last enemy of Christ. His lordship over creation will be manifest and undeniable as every tongue confesses "Jesus Christ is Lord" to the glory of God the Father. As Paul wrote, **Then comes the end, when he delivers the kingdom to God the Father after destroying every rule and every authority and power. For he must reign until he has put all his enemies under his feet. The last enemy to be destroyed is death** (1 Corinthians 15:24-26 ESV).

Part 3

Making Peace with God

You have been a refuge for the poor, a refuge for the needy in distress, a shelter from the storm and a shade from the heat. Isaiah 25:4 ESV

THE END OF THE CURSE IS AT HAND

Jesus invites everyone to come to him for eternal life, escaping the curse of death. He suffered the physical death of his body to redeem them who were "under the law of sin and death" (Romans 8:1,2). **But to all who did receive him, who believed in his name, he gave the right to become children of God, who were born, not of blood nor of the will of the flesh nor of the will of man, but of God** (John 1:12-13 ESV).

———————✝——————— He cancelled the prosecution of our sins that would have sent us to eternal punishment.

The elimination of the curse of death is given to those who believe in Jesus. The curse is ended the moment we bow to him who is "alive forevermore." We pass from death to life. **Truly, truly, I say to you, whoever hears my word and believes him who sent me has eternal life. He does not come into judgment but has passed from death to life** (John 5:24 ESV).

The death of Jesus on the cross paid the penalty for sins that we have committed. But that is not obvious unless more is known than the local news about a man being crucified. Three men were crucified the day Jesus died. What makes his death different? God nurtured the nation of Israel with prophetic preparation, national laws, and providential preservation to give us a context for the mission of Jesus as Savior of the world.

Many people when they heard of the crucifixion of Jesus have thought it was just another over-reach of Roman oppression in Israel. A revelation of God was required to understand that the death of Jesus for sinners was a planned event. Without that divine perspective, time and distance would have obscured its meaning from then until now. Jesus would not have been understood as different from many others who have spoken truth and been killed for it. But believers in Jesus have that revelation in their hearts.

The message of God was that the guilt of sinning earns a punishment in every life, in every culture and in every generation. Sinners have lost contact with God and are under the judgment of death, but the punishment of death is cancelled through Jesus laying down his life at the cross.

John the Baptist publicly announced that Jesus was "the Lamb of God" when Jesus first appeared at John's revival meetings. Jesus was cast in the role of an innocent sacrificial offering from his first introduction, drawing meaning for

> When Jesus died in his flesh and blood body, he died the flesh and blood death God required of Adam when he was judged.

his ministry from the history of Israel's sacrificial system. **For by a single offering he has perfected for all time those who are being sanctified** (Hebrews 10:14 ESV).

All Jews knew from their sacrificial laws that the innocent lamb gave its life because of the sinner's guilt before God. Today morality is being re-defined as the protection of the sinner's right to fulfill his lusts, even at the expense of the innocent. Clearly this is self-deification. People grow up with an attitude of entitlement. An objective standard of behavior is spoken against and disregarded when the person of God is forgotten. A well-known verse in the Old Testament described a time when the nation of Israel suffered from the loss of worship of God. **In those days there was no king in Israel. Everyone did what was right in his own eyes** (Judges 17:6 ESV).

John the baptizer preached against selfish living and called for repentance to God. He told soldiers not to bully people with their authority, and neither should tax collectors enrich themselves by adding fees to the amounts due. He warned the religious people not to trust in traditions but to focus on doing good, and he told the common people to have compassion to share food and clothing with the poor. He told all the people to look for God's Savior who was about to be revealed.

The proper preparation for his coming was to do works consistent with repentance and to make personal confession of sins to God.

Perhaps surprisingly, John said Jesus the Savior would be a sacrificial lamb rather than a roaring lion. However, Jesus would prove the power of his ministry with a triumph over sin and a flood of the Holy Spirit. John preached the upset of the old-world order by the Savior who was bringing the end of the curse to all who received him with a repentant heart. **But to all who did receive him, who believed in his name, he gave the right to become children of God, who were born, not of blood nor of the will of the flesh nor of the will of man, but of God** (John 1:12-13 ESV).

The burden on Jesus was the accomplishment of his mission to break the curse of death entrenched in the world. **I have a baptism to be baptized with, and how great is my distress until it is accomplished!** (Luke 12:50 ESV).

Jesus knew his life as the sacrificial lamb of God was directing a tidal wave of suffering at him, climaxing in his death for sinners. Our futures are never known until they happen, but the mission of the Son of God was prophetically clear to John: **Behold, the Lamb of God, who takes away the sin of the world!** (John 1:29 ESV).

THE GOSPEL OF PEACE

There was no doubt that John was a firebrand. He taught that Jesus would baptize us with fire. This was the fire of purification from sin. From ancient times the purification of metals was accomplished with fire. **This is the statute of the law that the LORD has commanded Moses: only the gold, the silver, the bronze, the iron, the tin, and the lead, everything that can stand the fire, you shall pass through the fire, and it shall be clean** (Numbers 31:21-23 ESV). Everyone who comes to God will be purified.

Fire as a symbol represents the holiness of God that destroys sin but also purifies sinners by burning off impurities. Fire is also a word used by Jesus to warn about eternal punishment, which is not redemptive but punitive (Mark 9:47-48). When Isaiah was called to be a prophet his filthy speech was cleansed by God in a vision of a burning coal from the altar of God that touched his lips. This touch of fire cleansed him so that he could speak for God. So, the idea of fire is used several ways in the Bible.

At the same time, the gospel of Jesus Christ was a message of peace with God (Acts 10:36). The word "gospel" did not represent hellfire but a call to peace after estrangement. Jesus was compelled by his mission to speak words of peace, healing, reconciliation, and hope. If estrangement from God brought death, then "peace through Jesus Christ" was the destruction of death, its removal from God's creation, and the restoration of the God-mankind relationship.

Jesus revealed his calling as a proclamation of peace in his first sermon at his hometown of Nazareth (Luke 4:16-21.) He said, "this scripture is fulfilled" because he was now present as the Word of God in the flesh. He implored all people to come to him to ease their burdens. He taught that his yoke is easy compared to the curse of sin and death. **Come to me, all who labor and are heavy laden, and I will give you rest. Take my yoke upon you, and learn from me, for I am gentle and lowly in heart, and you will find rest for your souls. For my yoke is easy, and my burden is light** (Matthew 11:28-30 ESV).

When Peter preached to the house of Cornelius after the resurrection of Jesus, he said that God sent the word to Israel **preaching good news of peace through Jesus Christ (he is Lord of all)** (Acts 10:36 ESV). He summed up the ministry of Jesus as the gospel of peace. Paul also summarized the gospel message as peace with God: **And he came and preached peace to you who were far off and peace to those who were near** (Ephesians 2:17 ESV). Both men taught the same message as was spoken by an angel at the birth of Jesus, **Glory to God in**

the highest, and on earth peace among those with whom he is pleased! (Luke 2:14 ESV).The prophet Isaiah ascribed the title Prince of Peace to Messiah (Isaiah 9:6).

The gospel is described as "preaching peace" because God is the one who has reached out to a world condemned to die. The apostle John wrote that all humanity is under the condemnation of death for sin. Into that bleak and broken world God has sent his Son to break us free. His initiative was an active force and this peace with God was the heart of the message of the Good News.

By the gospel of Jesus Christ, God is actively reaching out to us to come and receive the grace of God who has covered the debt of our estrangement. What will you do with the invitation?

ENTERING INTO GRACE BY FAITH

Eternal life begins personally not at the resurrection, but at the point of faith. Many Christians do not understand this truth and are merely hoping that everything will turn out well when they die. They are missing the confidence that God gives us now. This is revealed to us in the Bible where Paul wrote, **For by grace you have been saved through faith. And this is not your own doing; it is the gift of God, not a result of works, so that no one may boast** (Ephesians 2:8-9 ESV).

Some persons fear they must go through some post-death experience of spiritual rehabilitation after they die, but God says we are free from condemnation when we believe.

> **For God did not send his Son into the world to condemn the world, but in order that the world might be saved through him. Whoever believes in him is not condemned, but whoever does not believe is condemned already, because he has not believed in the name of the only Son of God.** John 3:17-18 ESV.

Do you see the transition here? The believer is now "not condemned", but the unbeliever is still under the curse of death for personal sins. To reverse the order, all persons are under condemnation until they believe in Jesus, and then the condemnation ceases.

Paul preached this when he wrote,

> **Therefore, if anyone is in Christ, he is a new creation. The old has passed away; behold, the new has come. All this is from God, who through Christ reconciled us to himself and gave us the ministry of reconciliation; that is, in Christ God was reconciling the world to himself, not counting their trespasses against them.** 2 Corinthians 5:17-19 ESV.

When a person believes in Jesus Christ as God's Son then the "new birth" in the heart has occurred. This is a legal reality regardless of our emotions, the objections of others, or even our mental shortcomings to comprehend the eternal implications of our conversion.

Paul wrote, "Behold, the new has come" because, like an iceberg in the ocean, most of the eternal miracle at work in us is hidden from view when we first believe in Jesus. "Behold" is the imperative Greek form of the verb "to see." It means "Look!" and "Open your eyes!" and "Give attention to what is happening here!" The old separation from God has ended. The new eternal relationship has begun.

When my son and his wife adopted a foster child, I was present in the courtroom. The judge was patient to explain that when she gives the order of adoption, the life of that child will be on a totally new legal path. She gave some examples, such as inheritance rights. She was saying, "Behold! From now on life is going to be different in ways you cannot see now because the law concerning you has changed." The child was less than five years old and although she could not compre-hend the change, it became true, nonetheless. **But, as it is written, "What no eye has seen, nor ear heard, nor the heart of man imagined, what God has prepared for those who love him"** (1 Corinthians 2:9 ESV).

THE INTERMEDIATE STATE OF THE DEAD

Naturally, if God has set a great white throne judgment at the end of this earth's history (Revelation 20:11-12), then there is some form of waiting state for the spirits of those who have died before the day of universal judgment. The Scriptures talk mostly about this present life and the final judgment to come rather than about the intermediate state between the death of the body and the resurrection when **all that are in the graves shall hear his voice** (John 5:28).

The intermediate state of the dead who are awaiting a res-urrection to life or a resurrection to the second death is a legit-imate topic to study, but of minor importance as far as final judgment and the two deaths is concerned. This is because our life in the flesh is the basis of the final judgment. We have no indication that anyone changes spiritually after the death of the body in the intermediate time awaiting Jesus's return. Jesus warned his hearers to deal with their sin before death (John 8:24). Our life is the sum of our deeds done during our lifetime before physical death (Revelation 20:12). For further personal study, the Bible student should look for references to *sheol* and *hades*, which are the Hebrew and Greek terms used for the place of the dead awaiting resurrection.

The works of a person include deeds done and beliefs held while alive. **Then they said to him, "What must we do, to be doing the works of God?" Jesus answered them, "This is the work of God, that you believe in him whom he has sent"** (John 6:28-29 ESV).

James said beliefs and deeds are so intertwined that they are one (James 2:22). The biblical basis for judgment is deeds done in our life in the flesh before physical death. After death there is a waiting period until Jesus returns, followed by the resurrection to life for believers in Jesus, or a resurrection to the post-death judgment ending in the second death for those who did not receive him as Lord (John 5:29). Believers' names are written in the Lamb's book of life (Revelation 20:12, 21:27). Because their sins are already confessed and forgiven, believers will not go through the sentencing judgment.

The references to the intermediate state are very few and support the view that intermediate states of the lost and the saved differ from each other and are in keeping with the two final states of life or death. The intermediate state of those who are united in faith to Jesus is paradise with God (Luke 23:43), while the state of the unrepentant is pain and isolation (Luke 16:25). Paul in Hebrews 9:27 skips over the intermediate state completely: **And just as it is appointed for man to die once, and after that comes judgment...** (Hebrews 9:27 ESV). Occasionally, he references it as an unnatural and temporary state because human beings are made for bodies, whether physical or resurrection types (2 Corinthians 5:1-4).

A person without a body is in an abnormal and unstable condition. In eternity every person created will have a body and not be a wispy spirit just floating around, as some imagine. Human beings are always differentiated from angels, and never take their form. Jesus, in an illustrative story, spoke of those who had recently died as separated and not intermixing with the living (Luke 16:26). In the book of Revelation, the spirits of the martyrs are impatiently waiting in a kind of divine rest, awaiting the unfolding of God's plan (Revelation 6:9-11).

Paul made it clear that at the resurrection we will be given a new resurrection body. Unlike our "natural" body, he said, it will be "spiritual" but still a "body." It may bear little resemblance to our present body. After all, even if an old friend has lost 50 or 100 pounds since we last saw them, they may be unrecognizable to us. Paul used the illustration of the dramatic change of a seed becoming a plant so that we would not limit our understanding of how God can work beyond our imagining.

We must look at the characteristics of Jesus after his resurrection for a comparison and as a starting point for understanding the resurrection. When he appeared to the disciples after his resurrection, Jesus was so healthy that he had to show Thomas the nail prints in his hands for him to believe. The scars of crucifixion were preserved as a witness of his love for us. God is not obliged to give us all the details. Nor is God forbidden from having our resurrection bodies change in the future. After all, we change now as we mature and age. Paul's discussion of the resurrection body is in 1 Corinthians 15:35-49.

Even in First Corinthians Paul does not speak of the intermediate state but focuses on our natural body and the body we receive at the time of the resurrection. The intermediate state is a very minor revelation in Scripture, so it is better to focus on this natural life and the promise of a resurrection body like Jesus received. This is what the Bible does. Eternal life with Jesus is the focus of the apostles.

EXEMPTION FROM THE SECOND DEATH

Listen to what Jesus said before he raised Lazarus back to life.

> **Jesus said to her, "Your brother will rise again."
> Martha said to him, "I know that he will rise
> again in the resurrection on the last day." Jesus
> said to her, "I am the resurrection and the life.
> Whoever believes in me, though he die, yet shall
> he live, and everyone who lives and believes in
> me shall never die."** John 11:23-26 ESV.

These words seem confusing, but Jesus is speaking of the first death, the second death, and eternal life. **Whoever believes**

in me, though he die, yet shall he live. Jesus was saying that if you believe in him, and your body dies, you will live in the resurrection of believers. This is the first death of the body. But then he says, **Everyone who lives and believes in me will never die.** This second time he is talking about living right through the death of the body experience and never dying the second death because we are given the gift of eternal life when we believe in Jesus. A.T. Robertson translated "will never die" as "shall not die forever" (Word Pictures in the New Testament). Everyone who lives and believes in Jesus will never die from the second death. To prove the truth of this teaching and his claim to be the author of life, Jesus then raised Lazarus from the dead physically.

Death is simply not a barrier to the power of God. Jesus became the first man with an eternal glorified body when he was raised from the dead (Colossians 1:18). When Jesus raised Lazarus, it was a return to a natural body. It was not yet the time for the resurrection of the righteous which is promised to occur at Jesus's return in power and glory (Revelation 20:4,5).

Martha was correct to believe as she did in the resurrection of Lazarus at the last day. Jesus restored the bodily life of Lazarus as a super healing back into natural life, but it was also an object lesson about the new life we received when we believed in him as Savior. **Everyone who lives and believes in me will never die.** Jesus expected people to understand that his power over the temporal world included power in the eternal realm.

The principle he was teaching when Jesus raised Lazarus was that victory over the second death is effective immediately for everyone that believes in him. This eternal life will persist through the death of the body, unhindered by it. Of course, we are respectful to the body of anyone who has died, but the person who was living there has moved on, so we don't talk to a dead body or hold it dear as a sacred object.

This eternal life is a gift. **For the wages of sin is death, but the free gift of God is eternal life in Christ Jesus our Lord** (Romans 6:23 ESV). With the gift comes an exemption from condemnation at the final judgment. **Blessed and holy is the one who shares in** the first resurrection! Over such the second death has no power, but they will be priests of God and of Christ, and they will reign with him for a thousand years (Revelation 20:6 ESV).

BELIEVERS IN JESUS DO NOT COME UNDER JUDGMENT

The primary danger of the curse of death is dying unforgiven in our sins. Grace is available only during our lifetime while we can repent and believe. After bodily death the process of condemnation under the curse of death given to Adam continues to the next step of the great white throne judgment. Without forgiveness in this life, the sentencing at the last judgment must end in a sentencing to the second death (Revelation 21:27).

The only way the believer can pass from death to life is faith in Jesus. Reconciliation to God means our sins are forgiven. Having received forgiveness, the worst outcome of physical life is removed. We cannot go to hell, which is the second death. We cannot die in our sins if we are forgiven because there is no remaining debt with God. In fact, just the opposite is true when we become the children of God. As Jesus said, **Truly, truly, I say to you, whoever hears my word and believes him who sent me has eternal life. He does not come into judgment, but has passed from death to life** (John 5:24 ESV).

At the great white throne judgment there is more than a single book mentioned by which the dead are judged. One is mentioned by name. In Revelation 21:27 it is called "The Lamb's book of life." Those written in the Lamb's Book are those who have received eternal life before they died. The rest are convicted of their own sinful deeds recorded in the other books (Revelation 20:12).

The believer's experience of death is completely different than the unbeliever. The present possession of eternal life assures us that we will not come into condemnation at a later judgment but are exempt.

Although we die physically, our experience of death is not under the curse. The fear is defanged, and the stinger is removed (Hebrews 2:14,15). The fear of death was based upon the judgment to follow, but we are now covered by Jesus's blood shed to death as our sacrifice, thus bringing peace with God.

Violent movies use make-up wounds with look-alike blood. A violent scene is portrayed by blood-splatter to heighten a sense of tragedy. In the Jewish sacrificial system, the blood was real and was sprinkled in varied ways according to the type of ritual. Moses commanded that a light sprinkling of the blood of the sacrificial animal be applied to the repentant offeror in one kind of sacrifice (Leviticus 14:7). It showed that the animal was slain, but the sinner was alive and forgiven, at the cost of a life. In the New Testament, this sacrificial language is used about Jesus dying for us on the cross, where he bled to death (Hebrews 12:24).

God has promised that we do not come into judgment. **For Christ also suffered once for sins, the righteous for the unrighteous, that he might bring us to God, being put to death in the flesh but made alive in the spirit** (1 Peter 3:18 ESV).

ENDING THE FEAR OF DEATH

Now that we have been given the gift of eternal life when we believed in Jesus, death has lost its power of fear.

> **Since therefore the children share in flesh and blood, he himself likewise partook of the same things, that through death he might destroy the one who has the power of death, that is, the devil, and deliver all those who through fear of death were subject to lifelong slavery.**
> Hebrews 2:14-15 ESV.

The power of fear is based upon the surety of the coming judgment for sins committed in this life. As our faith in what

————+———— Jesus has done for us grows, the fear of death fades.

As our faith in what Jesus has done for us grows, the fear of death fades.

By this is love perfected with us, so that we may have confidence for the day of judgment, because as he is so also are we in this world. There is no fear in love, but perfect love casts out fear. For fear has to do with punishment, and whoever fears has not been perfected in love. 1 John 4:17-18 ESV.

"In Adam all die" is the judgment the world is currently experiencing. God wants to wake everyone up to repentance before the sentencing of the second death. If the Son of God lived through death and is "alive forevermore" (Revelation 1:18), then death

————+————

Death is a bump in the road, not the dead-end of a road.

is a bump in the road, not the dead-end of a road.

In Matthew 10:25-28 Jesus said, **It is enough for the disciple to be like his teacher, and the servant like his master** (Matthew 10:25 ESV). He then proceeds seamlessly to speak of death by persecution. **And do not fear those who kill the body but cannot kill the soul** (Matthew 10:28 ESV). God allows us to follow Jesus in the experience of persecution even to death because that is what his Son endured.

God has taken the sting out of death because he has given us the gift of eternal life before we die. It is the gift of eternal life that carries us through death to our own resurrection. It supports us legally because our sins are forgiven, and it carries us emotionally because following Jesus in the hard times of persecutions will mean that we also will be like him in his resurrection. **For if we have been united with him in a death**

like his, we shall certainly be united with him in a resurrection like his (Romans 6:5 ESV).

The apostle John wrote, **Beloved, we are God's children now, and what we will be has not yet appeared; but we know that when he appears we shall be like him, because we shall see him as he is** (1 John 3:2 ESV). Paul wrote that his soon coming death would be his move onward to be with Christ, which is far better (Philippians 1:23). These two apostles were not discouraged at the thought of going through death because they were confident of God's resurrection promise.

Sin was judged on the cross, and God has promised us a victory that is assured by the resurrection of Jesus. As much as we all love instant answers, in real life God takes us through a growth process to future maturity.

> **And you, being dead in your sins and the uncircumcision of your flesh, He has made alive together with Him, having forgiven you all trespasses, blotting out the handwriting of ordinances that was against us, which was contrary to us, and has taken it out of the way, nailing it to the cross. Having stripped rulers and authorities, He made a show of them publicly, triumphing over them in it.** Colossians 2:13-15 MKJV.

The immediate benefit of faith is a deliverance from the fear of the unknowns of death. God does not want us to be a slave to our fears, but to live in fellowship with Jesus.

God has given us assurance that "death will be no more" in God's new heaven and earth (Revelation 21:4). After his own resurrection Jesus told John in a vision that through his death and resurrection, he now is victorious over death. **I died, and behold I am alive forevermore, and I have the keys of Death and Hades** (Revelation 1:18 ESV).

As the history of the earth unfolds, the timing of events is all in God's hands. Jesus told us beforehand that this is the way it will be. Jesus said that although we die in the body, it will be as though we did not die. Jesus said to Martha, **I am the resurrection and the life. Whoever believes in me, though he die, yet shall he live, and everyone who lives and believes in me shall never die. Do you believe this?** (John 11:25-26 ESV).

This is a very deep spiritual truth to believe. What can science offer? "We know your brain will stop, but we can't guarantee your spirit will stop. We haven't figured out what consciousness is yet." On the contrary, Jesus guarantees his defeat of death by the proofs of his own perfect life and miracles. **Do you not believe that I am in the Father and the Father in Me? The Words that I speak to you I do not speak of Myself, but the Father who dwells in Me, He does the works. Believe Me that I am in the Father and the Father in Me, or else believe Me for the very works themselves** (John 14:10-11 MKJV).

The fact that we believers die in the body is of secondary importance in God's view. This is not to say God does not care deeply, because at the grave of Lazarus, Jesus cried knowing full well he was about to raise him from the dead! The Psalmist declared, **Precious in the sight of the LORD is the death of his saints** (Psalms 116:15 KJV).

Jesus had two important teachings about the fear of dying. First, he put the death of the body in perspective by teaching about the more important subject of our eternal state. **You are from below; I am from above. You are of this world; I am not of this world. I told you that you would die in your sins, for unless you believe that I am he you will die in your sins** (John 8:23-24 ESV). He was not as concerned with the death of the body as much as he was concerned with the spiritual state of the person at death, whether they were a believer or an unbeliever in himself.

The second teaching confirms the first and is found in Luke 12. **I tell you, my friends, do not fear those who kill the body, and after that have nothing more that they can do. But I will warn you whom to fear: fear him who, after he has killed, has authority to cast into hell. Yes, I tell you, fear him!**

(Luke 12:4-5 ESV).Persecutions are limited, but hell is never ending. Focusing
on the life to be lived after this life puts
this life in the proper perspective.

Focusing on the life to be lived after this life puts this life in the proper perspective.

Jesus is less concerned about
his believers ("my friends") experiencing physical death than he is about
them staying faithful and believing.
By staying faithful they will avoid the
second death. To unbelievers he acknowledges that there are
two deaths that result from Adam's judgment. He therefore
warns them to repent and believe in him as Messiah.

We must conclude that the death of a believer is not due
to condemnation for his past sins, now covered by the sacrifice of Christ, but because of the residual curse on all creation.
The last enemy to be destroyed is death, Paul wrote in First
Corinthians (1 Corinthians 15:26 ESV). John had the same revelation. **He will wipe away every tear from their eyes, and
death shall be no more, neither shall there be mourning, nor
crying, nor pain anymore, for the former things have passed
away** (Revelation 21:4 ESV).Until then the creation is still
groaning awaiting liberation from the judgment of death by
the liberated sons of God (Romans 8:21).

When God allows believers to go through physical death, the
victory of Jesus is re-played in their lives. Like Jesus, a believer
who is joined to Christ will say, "I was dead, but look—I am alive
forever and ever!" (Revelation 1:18 TLV). They are strengthened
because they have taken the devil's worst and turned it into the
victory of God by their union with Christ (Hebrews 2:14).

Paul viewed his own sufferings and death, not as a judgment, but as a union with Christ's sufferings that were redemptive. **Now I rejoice in my sufferings for your sake, and in my
flesh I am filling up what is lacking in Christ's afflictions for
the sake of his body, that is, the church** (Colossians 1:24 ESV).

He saw the continuation of his life until the end as an opportunity to be involved in Christ's work (2 Corinthians 6:1). We should follow Paul's example in whose estimation death was defeated.

Jesus spoke of the death of the body as merely the last connection with persecution (Luke 12:4). In the spiritual fight of faith, Jesus said that the death of the body was a permanent escape. At the death of the body a believer leaves behind a time-limited and finite persecution for an untimed eternal life with God. The unbeliever, however, cannot rest knowing that at the end of this life there awaits the eternal condemnation of the second death. That fear enslaves the soul (Hebrews 2:15).

Deliverance from the fear of death was demonstrated in the grandfather of a friend of mine. Every year the family gathered at his home in a small farming community. Even in his old age he kept serving his home church by doing chores and mowing the lawn. At family reunions he would rejoice he was getting on in years and was going to see Jesus. This was distressing to some of the family when he seemed to treat death lightly, but he said he had true faith and was really looking forward to heaven.

Eventually he died rather suddenly, and the family gathered at the church for a funeral service. He had died so suddenly that the church lawn was cut for his funeral by himself. If that makes you smile, it is because Jesus is teaching you not to fear death. But if that makes you cringe, God still has something to teach you about his victory over death.

Perhaps the analogy of Esther in the Bible will grant us some courage. A new law of the Persians, although facetiously obtained by Haman, condemned the Jews in Persia to death at the hands of their enemies. Their only recourse was a second law granting them the right to fight back. Esther interceded before the King and was granted that contravening law, so the Jewish community took to the offense and survived (Esther 8:11).

God has given the believer his assurance that death will not win in this life because **though he die, yet shall he live** (John 11:25). In another place Paul wrote, **After disarming the** principalities and powers, He made a public spectacle of them, triumphing over them in the cross (Colossians 2:15 TLV). Jesus died in faith (Luke 23:46). Paul called it a "triumph."

Many people wear "the empty cross" as jewelry. This is not because they love execution. Jesus turned the death of the cross into the glory of the resurrection. The suffering of the cross is in the past and the grave is empty. Jesus proved that his life conquered death despite the cross. Peter preached, **God raised him up, loosing the pangs of death, because it was not possible for him to be held by it** (Acts 2:24 ESV).

THE SPIRITUAL NEW BIRTH

The work of God in a person's life is a truly remarkable event. Jesus called it a new birth (John 3). This is where the expression "born again Christian" comes from. The "born again" experience is a conversion of belief based upon personal faith in Jesus Christ, believing in his eternal sonship to our Father God in heaven, and in his resurrection and continued existence as the Savior of the world. We also receive the gift of eternal life at conversion. This is the beginning of a new life that rises out of the ashes of the old. These are the spiritual realities that do not fit neatly into traditional psychological and sociological constructs.

The lordship of Jesus is more than adherence to facts about his life. The lordship of Jesus is submission with worship to the living and eternal God, our Creator, every day of our lives. People are still individuals, and some persons are radically changed in their behavior in a day. Others take longer to sort out their behaviors under the lordship of Christ. The church of Jesus is not a militarized body of recruits, but individuals growing at their own speed. Nevertheless, the new life takes form and is a witness to others and to their own selves that they have been "born again."

The new birth begins at a singular moment of time in our life when we personally receive by faith the lordship of Jesus Christ.

From that point on our relationship with God is ongoing, being a living relationship built upon spiritual fellowship with God. Jesus told the woman at the well, **God is spirit, and those who worship him must worship in spirit and truth** (John 4:24 ESV).

When God speaks in the Bible about faith, He refers to a belief grounded in our whole personality. Jesus said, **And you shall love the Lord your God with all your heart and with all your soul and with all your mind and with all your strength** (Mark 12:30 ESV). Faith is not meant to be a spiritual experience separate from the rest of our lives.

Conversion is essentially a personal revelation of Jesus wherein the individual finds his identity "in Christ," because the believer becomes aware of the living God who is present in his life. Prayer to God becomes personal rather than reading a prayer from a book. This personal revelation is repeated in all others who are born again, so that no one can claim an exclusive experience with God.

THE CHURCH

Neither is faith in Jesus merely a subjective experience. Experience and education work together in the life of a Christian. Jesus said, **If anyone's will is to do God's will, he will know whether the teaching is from God or whether I am speaking on my own authority** (John 7:17 ESV). The community of faith (the local church) is instrumental in both education and experience because God is kingdom-centered in his purpose. We are not meant to be alone, but in a community whenever possible.

———+———

Experience and education work together in the life of a Christian.

As individuals speak of their experiences, they assist the growth of the others because walking by faith is also the common experience of others. We learn we are not alone.

All believers are bound together "in Christ." Paul used the metaphor of the church being a body with many different members, but united with a single head, the risen Lord Jesus, **from whom the whole body, joined and held together by every joint with which it is equipped, when each part is working properly, makes the body grow so that it builds itself up in love** (Ephesians 4:16 ESV).

When Peter first confessed his faith in Jesus as the Christ, Jesus responded with a prophecy about the church. A church is simply a gathering of believers in Jesus who regularly meet as an assembly to worship their Lord. Jesus said, **Blessed are you, Simon Bar-Jonah! For flesh and blood has not revealed this to you, but my Father who is in heaven. And I tell you, you are Peter, and on this rock I will build my church, and the gates of hell shall not prevail against it** (Matthew 16:17-18 ESV).

The word "church" in the New Testament did not refer to a religious corporation but an assembly of persons sharing the experience of new birth and functioning as the Holy Spirit had gifted them for mutual growth.

Jesus explained the new birth to Nicodemus, a Jewish theologian, when he said, **Truly, truly, I say to you, unless one is born again, he cannot see the kingdom of God** (John 3:3 ESV). If you are born-again, you should accept that God works through believers in a community of faith. The same Spirit who gives the personal experience of conversion to you is at the same time giving a revelation of community so that we can "see the kingdom." Pray that God will show you a local church where He wants you to thrive.

The "born again" experience is highly personal, yet the kingdom of God unifies individual experiences into corporate worship of the one true God. Having the personal experience opens our hearts and minds to the kingdom of God, the community of all who have had the personal re-birth that comes with faith.

The emphasis in the local church is not on the organization, but on the rule of God in the world by the Lord of all, Jesus Christ.

There is one true Lord, and so there can only be one kingdom of God. The local church is a local expression of the broader domain of the kingdom of God. In this way the local assembly is a living prophecy of the coming universal reign of God in the earth.

The local church must be physically gathered together because God is working in the gifts of the Holy Spirit as He anoints individuals to benefit the whole group. **To each is given the manifestation of the Spirit for the common good** (1 Corinthians 12:7 ESV).

The study of Christian believers living united in faith is called "ecclesiology," the study of the church of Jesus. Yes, all churches experience imperfect relationships. We all have had times when we wished we did not have to work at perfecting relationships with others. Dealing with our own weaknesses and imperfections is a full-time job! Nevertheless, God chooses to organize us as a local community. His Spirit is given differently to each of us to build up the whole. Like gemstones in a tumbler, he keeps us in constant contact with others to perfect our character until it shines. Jesus is building a kingdom to glorify God.

UNION WITH CHRIST

A changed life is possible because Jesus broke the power of sin by dying on the cross as an offering well pleasing to God. We identify with the Messiah who "died for our sins" first by faith in him and secondly by experience. Paul told Timothy, **I am not ashamed, for I know whom I have believed, and I am convinced that he is able to guard until that Day what has been entrusted to me** (2 Timothy 1:12 ESV).

You must realize that you died with Christ before you can live with Christ.

Christianity is more than merely identifying with a noble cause. Paul wrote, **we are dead with Christ** (Romans 6:8). Do not try to live out your new life in Christ with the old habits. You must realize that you *died* with Christ before you can *live* with Christ. Behind every conversion to Christ is a conviction of heart that has determined to break with the past. Faith is more real to the Christian than mental ascent, cultural ties, social pressure, or past sins that pleased only our own selves.

God brings us into a union with Himself, so that from the moment of spiritual birth we are legally "in Christ." As the only true sinless individual in the history of the world, Jesus had the virtue to offer his physical death to break the curse of death that held us. From that point forward, there are a multitude of "benefits." God's life in us is forever blossoming. **For if while we were enemies we were reconciled to God by the death of his Son, much more, now that we are reconciled, shall we be saved by his life** (Romans 5:10 ESV).

The single offering of the body of Jesus Christ to taste death for us has both brought forgiveness of sins and a new nature to us. Paul wrote, **put on the new self, created after the likeness of God in true righteousness and holiness** (Ephesians 4:24 ESV). The end of our past life is founded upon forgiveness, and the beginning of our future is a newness of life only possible by God's life in Jesus Christ placed within us.

Therefore, if any man be in Christ, he is a new creature: old things are passed away; behold, all things are become new (2 Corinthians 5:17 KJV). Paul presented holy living not as a restriction of freedoms but as an expression of thanksgiving to God for being set free from enslavement to sin. **We know that our old self was crucified with him in order that the body of sin might be brought to nothing, so that we would no longer be enslaved to sin. For one who has died has been set free from sin** (Romans 6:6-7 ESV).

> Paul presented holy living not as a restriction of freedoms but as an expression of thanksgiving to God.

THE END OF THE OLD LIFE

The life of an unbeliever is not to be envied. The person who does not live under the lordship of Jesus is "already condemned" (John 3:18). The apostle Paul said that unbelieving people are living without hope and without God because the sentence of death remains over them (Ephesians 2:11 – 22).

That is no way to live, but multitudes are living their lives under the curse. They seek a cure for a life of godlessness and hopelessness by trying to have fun, be creative, build human relationships, hoard possessions, increase education, and travel. Sadly, when these are not available, they seek to escape their pain with alcohol, drugs, neuroses, dual personalities, denial, psychoses, idolatries, or just giving up on life in a general depression because they do not know where to turn for relief. Life becomes a race against time with increasing disability of mind and body. Blessed is the one who comes to God with this life of God in their youth!

The person who is born again meets God with worship and presents their self with an attitude of humility to process the required changes. Being united to Jesus Christ by faith, the Spirit of God within us witnesses that God is real. **But when the fullness of time had come, God sent forth his Son, born of woman, born under the law, to redeem those who were under the law, so that we might receive adoption as sons. And because you are sons, God has sent the Spirit of his Son into our hearts, crying, "Abba! Father!"** (Galatians 4:4-6 ESV).

This new relationship with God is the result of the breaking of the curse of death over our lives. Jesus has died a real death sentence for the guilty who now believe in him. Such faith has an immediate impact upon a person. The individual stands acquitted before God. The burden of finding meaning

This new relationship with God is the result of the breaking of the curse of death over our lives.

now shifts from looking at temporal fixes to a growing relationship with the Creator.

The corollaries of the curse of death begin to fade as we *grow*. Jesus said he has come so that we can experience life "more abundantly" (John 10:10). This speaks not of stagnation but an ever-increasing fulness of life. An over-emphasis on being "born-again" as a status yields the prideful attitude of "us versus them." We should understand that we are "born-again" to "grow-anew." A person who is always growing is humbled that he is not "there" yet.

THE OPPORTUNITY FOR REPENTANCE

The imposition of death in two stages, physical and eternal, allowed God to give all sinful humans an opportunity to repent. **The Lord is not slow concerning His promise, as some count slowness, but is long-suffering toward us, not purposing that any should perish, but that all should come to repentance** (2 Peter 3:9 MKJV). The only time to get right with God is now in this physical life. Sinners are living on borrowed time, already convicted.

I mentioned before the "divine forbearance" of God. **Because in his divine forbearance he had passed over former sins** (Romans 3:25 ESV). Do not confuse the grace of God which delays judgment for a universal cancellation of judgment. Faith never comes by accident or involuntarily. The gospel is never to be preached as self-enlightenment: "Look deep within and you will see the light of truth." God is commanding all people to repent, stop sinning and start worshipping. I liked the church street sign I saw that read, "Believe, Belong, Behave."

God requires all persons to examine themselves because repentance must occur in this life before death comes. There is no opportunity for repentance

> Faith never comes by accident or involuntarily.

after death. The urgency for repentance comes from several directions, including Moses and the prophets (Luke 16:31), our consciences (Romans 2:15), the gospel (Mark 1:15), and the inner conviction of the Holy Spirit (John 16:7,8).

The curse of death is dying. Every life is under the curse of death until a person comes to God through Jesus: **I am the way, and the truth, and the life. No one comes to the Father except through me** (John 14:6 ESV).

Some persons have decades of time to repent, and some have much less; we never know which until death comes. Repentance must occur in this life or we will die in our sins, meaning there is no further opportunity to reconcile with God. "Dying in your sins" (John 8:24) locks a person in their present condemnation (John 3:18), and therefore into a future judgment that will end in the second death at the great white throne judgment of God (Revelation 20:11).

God leads sinners to repentance by showing them the shallowness of life without faith. He or she is born estranged from God, but with an unquenchable thirst for spiritual life. That person gets a taste of love and is frustrated with the shortness of life to express it. God sends the gospel call to repent and come to Jesus to receive forgiveness, because the Savior in love has paid the price for sins. If a sinner refuses to reconcile, then he dies "without Christ" and is locked into a resurrection awaiting condemnation for his sins at the last judgment (John 5:29). That will be the second death of eternal punishment.

The case of the repentant sinner is entirely different. He or she is under "the same condemnation" of a brief time to live. We have the example of the two men who were crucified beside Jesus (Luke 23:40). One repented and believed in Jesus and his coming kingdom, contrary to all physical evidence. He did not "die in his sins." The other man did.

Jesus taught alternate outcomes for believers and unbelievers in John chapter 8. Those who believe in Messiah receive him into their life as Lord and Savior. Making Jesus Lord means one has repented, turned his life over to God, and taken up his cross daily to follow in Jesus's steps (John 13:14,15). Many suggest a prayer that specifically asks, "Oh God, I turn from my old life and ask your forgiveness. I believe Jesus died to pay for my sins. I receive you, Lord Jesus, as my Lord and Savior." Anything like that will do. There is no perfect prayer; just speak from your heart to God.

THE WRATH OF GOD IS COMING

John the baptizer was not shy about "telling it like it is." When the religious professionals of his day showed up at the river, he said, **You brood of vipers! Who warned you to flee from the wrath to come?** (Matthew 3:7 ESV).

When we read about the "wrath of God" to come, it is not a new judgment. It is the same curse of death on Adam, delayed in implementation by God to allow time for repentance. Peter clearly wrote that the wrath of God is delayed, being "stored up" for a release at a future time. **But by the same word the heavens and earth that now exist are stored up for fire, being kept until the day of judgment and destruction of the ungodly** (2 Peter 3:7 ESV).

Jesus acknowledged in his teachings that the wicked are not immediately judged. In many parables he spoke of the longsuffering of God. One parable talked about repeated attempts of a king to be recognized as sovereign, or in another story he told about an attempt at fertilizing a non-producing tree before cutting it down. In another parable he spoke of the delay in uprooting weeds interspersed with growing wheat. These all speak of the forbearance of God. Remember, forbearance is a delay but not a cancellation of the wages of sin. The wrath of God is coming.

When Paul preached in Athens, he mentioned the delay of judgment. He explained,

> **The times of ignorance God overlooked, but now he commands all people everywhere to**

> **repent, because he has fixed a day on which he will judge the world in righteousness by a man whom he has appointed; and of this he has given assurance to all by raising him from the dead.** Acts 17:30-31 ESV.

We should not think the word translated "overlooked" means "excused." Paul believed the entire world was already guilty under the judgment of God that came from Adam's sin. Paul used the word "overlooked" (King James: "winked at") in the context of a future day of reckoning. In effect, he was saying that God is long-suffering by not demanding payment for our sins *immediately*.

Compare this "delay" of judgment to Exodus 34:6,7 where God said he **forgives iniquity, rebellion, and sin, but by no means clears the guilty.** The forgiveness of God came not by fiat but by satisfaction through a payment of the debt of death by another who died in the place of the sinner. This is why "Jesus died for our sins" is often repeated in the New Testament.

In all these ways, God was delaying their earned judgment a while longer, but in no way was ignoring or universally cancelling past sins. His purpose was to lead sinners to repent before they die and to receive forgiveness, because after death there is no opportunity for repentance before the final great judgment for which God has already set a date.

THE PLACE FOR GRACE

The word "grace" is used frequently in the Bible. The famous song "Amazing Grace" is so popular because of the abundant relief it brings from the anxiety commonly experienced by believers in Jesus. The grace of God replaces an experience of lostness with one of comforting welcome into a kingdom full of other people on the same journey in the community of faith in Jesus.

The word "grace" referred to a warm and fuzzy feeling in the classical Greek, but increasingly in Christian usage it referred to the warm welcome God provided to sinful humans who do not deserve a second chance to mend their ways. God, in love, repeatedly gives us opportunity for repentance. Hopefully, the definition of grace will not return to simply warm and fuzzy feelings that may arise regardless of true change.

Grace extends a welcoming invitation to reconcile with God before his wrath is revealed. Grace always surprises us because we do not expect kindness from someone we have greatly offended. **Therefore, we are ambassadors for Christ, God making his appeal through us. We implore you on behalf of Christ, be reconciled to God** (2 Corinthians 5:20 ESV).

Grace is amazing because God had already been so offended by mankind's sinning that he has placed us under the curse of death. Now He wants us to receive the gift of life through Jesus. Remember this: his curse of death was not raw anger, but a judgment brought upon us by our own sins. Although that righteous sentence of death was declared in Genesis 3, He offers a way out of death without pre-conditions or qualifications. God always says, 'Come now' and "Come as you are" and "Come to change."

> Grace is amazing because God had already been so offended by mankind's sinning that he has placed us under the curse of death.

His forgiveness is based upon a payment made by another person. You do not have to be famous or rich or pretty or smart. The initiative here is all on God's part. **For from his fullness we have all received, grace upon grace. For the law was given through Moses; grace and truth came through Jesus Christ** (John 1:16-17 ESV).

> You do not have to be famous or rich or pretty or smart. The initiative here is all on God's part.

In his gospel book, John was presenting the wondrous love of the God who took on the same flesh and blood as the humans He had made. He sought them out in the person of his unique Son Jesus on their own turf on the earth, instead of remaining in a distant and unreachable heaven. Jesus taught, **You are from below; I am from above. You are of this world; I am not of this world** (John 8:23 ESV). And yet, here he was on earth talking to them! More than that, God was and is still offering forgiveness to those already condemned, in a last attempt to avoid the time of judgment fixed in the future. **But God shows his love for us in that while we were still sinners, Christ died for us** (Romans 5:8 ESV).

See how grace and love are so closely related. Grace is the offer of reconciliation to obstinate and ornery people who do not deserve it. God by love offers grace as his campaign of "shock and awe," instead of lightning bolts and pitchforks of pain.

> **You have heard that it was said, "You shall love your neighbor and hate your enemy." But I say to you, love your enemies and pray for those who persecute you, so that you may be sons of your Father who is in heaven. For he makes his sun rise on the evil and on the good and sends rain on the just and on the unjust.**
>
> Matthew 5:43-45 ESV.

But remember that as amazing as grace is, it has an expiration date. All great sales and special offers have expiration dates, and so does the grace of God. The grace of God is his open invitation to put your faith in Jesus Christ as Lord and Savior. Paul's mission was to make this gracious invitation known. **We are therefore ambassadors for Messiah, as though God were making His appeal through us. We beg you on behalf of Messiah, be reconciled to God. He made the One who knew no sin to become a sin offering on our behalf, so that in Him we might become the righteousness of God** (2 Corinthians 5:20-21 TLV).

RECEIVING ETERNAL LIFE

When Jesus's substitutionary death on the cross is believed and received, the legal power of the curse of physical death is broken. Believers are restored to a personal relationship with God by faith. Because the curse is broken, they cannot die "in their sins," that is, guilty and already condemned.

Therefore, the moment a person believes in Jesus, eternal life begins (John 3:7). **Truly, truly, I say to you, whoever hears my word and believes him who sent me has eternal life. He does not come into judgment, but has passed from death to life** (John 5:24 ESV).

When Jesus says, "He does not come into judgment" he means the repentant sinner will not die unforgiven and face the great judgment at the end of time. Cancellation of the curse of death while a person is alive in this world is the guarantee that a future judgment of the second death does not apply when a believer dies. That is why Jesus said the believer **has passed from death to life**.

A rough analogy may be made to a sport team that has a lock on their playoff spot before the regular season ends. They still play games but are locked into the final playoff rounds mathematically. Having the possession of eternal life before death is the cause of Christians rejoicing in their salvation because Jesus said, **He does not come into judgment**.

The curse is broken because the sinner's punishment of death was paid by Jesus's death on the cross. Just as the virtue of Jesus spiritually flowed from Jesus's body into the woman who touched the hem of his garment seeking her healing, there is today virtue in Jesus because of his death for all who put their faith in him (Mark 5:25-34). Jesus is risen from the dead to make it happen for you, too.

As believers we experience the breaking of the curse as a death to our own past. Being "born again" requires a death of the past so that the new life may come to the fore. Jesus used the example of storing wine to illustrate the needed change. He said the old wineskins were dried out and could not bear the expansive fermentation of the new wine without breaking. New wineskin bottles were required. When we believe in the death of Christ on our behalf, we must accept a corresponding death within ourselves of our old ways that makes room for the new life in Christ.

If we are so bold as to ask God for forgiveness at the cost of Jesus's death, then we must accept a death of our old sinful self as a reasonable loss. **I appeal to you therefore, brothers, by the mercies of God, to present your bodies as a living sacrifice, holy and acceptable to God, which is your spiritual worship** (Romans 12:1 ESV).

Because it is not a physical death like martyrdom, this loss of putting aside our old life is sometimes overlooked. **What shall we say then? Are we to continue in sin that grace may abound? By no means! How can we who died to sin still live in it?** (Romans 6:1-2 ESV). Paul often mentioned that our union with Christ initiates both a break with the past as well as a future maturity in Christlikeness. If the new birth is the beginning of eternal life, then it is also the death of our old life. You cannot have one and keep the other when the curse is broken.

If the new birth is the beginning of eternal life, then it is also the death of our old life.

WHEN IS THE CURSE BROKEN?

The good news of Jesus is that the curse is broken. When? The moment we believe in Jesus, is the answer. The judgment of death is real. All people have died since Adam. People who "die in their sins" await a sure condemnation of second death at the great white throne judgment (Revelation 20). But a repentant sinner is immediately forgiven upon repentance and faith, and a future condemnation is cancelled.

The apostle John wrote that there is a new birth of life with God when a sinner repents. **But to all who did receive him, who believed in his name, he gave the right to become children of God, who were born, not of blood nor of the will of the flesh nor of the will of man, but of God** (John 1:12-13 ESV).

When any person believes in Jesus their sins are forgiven and they no longer "die in their sins" when they physically die. If a person can no longer die in their sins because they are beneficiaries of the blood sacrifice of Jesus, then they are not liable to the second death judgment after Jesus returns to earth. Therefore, we say Christians are "saved" because they are no longer subject to the future judgment of God.

> **For God so loved the world that He gave His only-begotten Son, that whoever believes in Him should not perish but have everlasting life. For God did not send His Son into the world to condemn the world, but so that the world might be saved through Him. He who believes on Him is not condemned, but he who does not believe is condemned already, because he has not believed in the name of the only-begotten Son of God.** John 3:16-18 MKJV.

Notice that John wrote, **He who believes on Him is not condemned, but he who does not believe is condemned already.** And he wrote that Jesus said, **Truly, truly, I say to you, He who hears My Word and believes on Him who sent Me has everlasting life and shall not come into condemnation but has passed from death to life** (John 5:24 MKJV).

> **Do not marvel at this, for the hour is coming in which all who are in the graves shall hear His voice, and shall come forth, those who**

have done good to the resurrection of life, and those who have practiced evil to the resurrection of condemnation. John 5:28-29 MKJV.

He who believes on the Son has everlasting life, and he who does not believe the Son shall not see life, but the wrath of God abides upon him John 3:36 MKJV.

Those who believe in Jesus accept his substitutionary atonement by believing the death that sinners deserved was placed upon another person, Jesus Christ. They allow themselves to be washed of their sins by the provision of God. It is good to use the terms precisely: "accept his death as your deliverance", and "receive Jesus as living Lord over your life". "Acceptance" is acknowledgment of truth. "Receiving" is the initiation of a personal relationship with Jeus who is raised from the dead and alive.

Sinners who repent have taken personal responsibility for their sins. They acknowledge the righteousness of God when He pronounced a curse of death on the world. Sinners under conviction of sin narrow their focus from all sinners to themselves. Each person understands that Jesus was on the cross for the guilt of their own sin.

God requires every individual to get personal and not be distracted with their neighbor's sins. In the sermon on the mount Jesus said, **Why do you see the speck that is in your brother's eye, but do not notice the log that is in your own eye?** (Luke 6:41 ESV). We cannot wait for others to repent. We must respond when God's Spirit convicts us.

Believers benefit by immediately receiving eternal life as a gift from God. This includes the cancellation of the personal legal liability of "dying in sins" when they repent. Death will end a person's deeds on earth, and repentance must happen before death. The time for repentance is today. **As it is said,**

"Today, if you hear his voice, do not harden your hearts" (Hebrews 3:15 ESV).

The merits of Jesus alone are why we are forgiven. No one comes to God feeling self-confident. All the verses just quoted say that the condemnation is cancelled for believers by the cost Jesus paid, but the alternative pathway for the unforgiven is surely the second death. The wrath of God is presently on them. Without forgiveness for a person's sins against God in this life, the second death is inescapable.

ETERNAL LIFE STARTS NOW

Jesus, John, and Paul were all in agreement on how God works. All liability for the sentence of the second death is ended when a believer puts their faith in Jesus as the Savior. Forgiven persons have no liability for past sins when they die, therefore they are not locked into condemnation at the final judgment. Death for a believer is merely a transition from one form of life to the next. Eternal life carries forgiven believers right through to "the other side." Because eternal life began at our spiritual new birth, our life does not change at physical death, only our body does.

I suppose I have to re-state the obvious truth that no person who is truly under the Lordship of Jesus will boast that they can sin with impunity after repentance. Such an attitude is a witness to a glaring fault in discipleship. As Paul wrote, **What shall we say then? Are we to continue in sin that grace may abound? By no means! How can we who died to sin still live in it?** (Romans 6:1-2 ESV).

> Because eternal life began at our spiritual new birth, our life does not change at physical death, only our body does.

In these words, we can almost hear Paul's sputtering exasperation at such a cavalier attitude toward sin. There is always grace for our failures, inadequacies, and shortcomings, but only if we live every day with a humble and repentant attitude toward God. This is what Jesus taught when he washed the feet of the disciples the night before he died (John 13:1-11).

Jesus plainly taught that we could have an assurance of our salvation. **Truly, truly, I say to you, whoever hears my word and believes him who sent me has eternal life. He does not come into judgment but has passed from death to life** (John 5:24 ESV).

> **Jesus then said, I am the one who raises the dead to life! Everyone who has faith in me will live, even if they die. And everyone who lives because of faith in me will never really die. Do you believe this?** John 11:25-26 CEV.

These extraordinary words translated here as "never really die" are even stronger in the original language where the Greek has six words. A more literal translation reads "never ever will die for ever." Jesus said that although a person experiences physical death, it will not be an eternal death. This is a direct reference to exemption from the final judgement that will result in the "second death" for unbelievers.

If we never die, but our body does die, then Jesus was teaching that our life is more than the living body we are in now. The consciousness of our spirit will continue after our body dies. Near the point of death on the cross Jesus gave comforting words to the repentant thief dying on the cross next to his own. He said, **Truly, I say to you, today you will be with me in Paradise** (Luke 23:43 ESV).

Paul wrote that it is not God's purpose to leave us without a body for eternity. Jesus waited to be raised on the third day after his bodily death, but Peter preached that **God raised him up, loosing the pangs of death, because it was not possible for him to be held by it** (Acts 2:24 ESV). Like Jesus, our eternal life will be accompanied by an eternal body, provided on God's timetable. Paul called it a "spiritual body" as opposed to one powered through circulating blood.

The resurrection of Jesus is the assurance of our resurrection. As John wrote, **Beloved, we are God's children now, and what we will be has not yet appeared; but we know that when he appears we shall be like him, because we shall see him as he is** (1 John 3:2 ESV).

A RESURRECTION TO LIFE

Neither Paul nor John gave us a detailed description of the resurrection body. Paul said that dying was like planting a seed. The plant grows out of the seed but bears no resemblance to a seed.

The physical life we have now is dominated by our natural senses. The life of the resurrection is a spiritually empowered body. Paul wrote that this future reality has no comparison to life as we now know it, although both are called "bodies." **Just as we have borne the image of the man of dust, we shall also bear the image of the man of heaven. I tell you this, brothers: flesh and blood cannot inherit the kingdom of God, nor does the perishable inherit the imperishable** (1 Corinthians 15:49-50 ESV).

Yes, people still grow old and die until Jesus returns. But this is not dying with the guilt of sins upon them. The death of the body continues for now because the whole creation was cursed when Adam sinned (Genesis 3:17). The cycle of death has infected all the cosmos because of Adam. After Jesus's example, a new world order is coming.

As the curse of death came on the earth in stages, God will remove it in stages. When Paul explained the resurrection, he used the phrase "each in his own order" (1 Corinthians 15:23). The redemption of the body from death will first be the privilege of believers in Christ before the full removal of death from all creation.

> When the perishable puts on the imperishable,
> and the mortal puts on immortality, then shall
> come to pass the saying that is written: "Death
> is swallowed up in victory." "O death, where
> is your victory? O death, where is your sting?"
> The sting of death is sin, and the power of sin
> is the law. But thanks be to God, who gives us
> the victory through our Lord Jesus Christ.
> 1 Corinthians 15:54-57 ESV.

Paul wrote that this truth should change our attitude now as believers in Jesus, while we wait for the kingdom of God to come in fulness. The next verse in this passage reads, **Therefore, my beloved brothers, be steadfast, immovable, always abounding in the work of the Lord, knowing that in the Lord your labor is not in vain** (1 Corinthians 15:58 ESV). The hope of future resurrection gives purpose to our current labors.

John simply said that we will be like Jesus. **Beloved, we are God's children now, and what we will be has not yet appeared; but we know that when he appears we shall be like him, because we shall see him as he is. And everyone who thus hopes in him purifies himself as he is pure** (1 John 3:2-3 ESV).

John said we can use that hope of a new body as motivation to live like Christ now. I wrote before about the sports team that had secured a playoff spot because of their winning record. We all know that they do not stop working hard. Practicing bad habits ends poorly. The same applies to the Christian's attitude toward his salvation in Christ. We pray for God to show us the good deeds He has prepared for us.

OBJECTIONS ANSWERED

Someone may object by saying, "But the believer is still going to die at the end of his life, and you say the curse of death is physical. So, is the curse removed or not?" I actually said that the curse is death in the physical *and* eternal dimensions. God's plan includes it all, and the deliverance comes in stages.

Paul clearly taught that the coming of the kingdom of God was progressing in stages. **For he must reign until he has put all his enemies under his feet** (1 Corinthians 15:25 ESV). In 1 Corinthians 15, the last days events were listed in order by Paul because there is much yet to unfold in God's plan of redemption.

If Jesus bore the physical death we deserve, why do we still grow old and die? Martha faced the same questions when her brother Lazarus died. Jesus did not arrive in time to heal him. But when he did arrive, she stated that her faith would not waiver no matter what questions she had about him dying while the Savior was on earth (John 11:17-44).

On two occasions Jesus spoke of death as if it were sleep, showing that he viewed death differently than an end of life. His word choice of "sleep" probably was prompted by the prophecy of Daniel (Daniel 12:2). Our sleep is a pause in activity, but not an end of life. Jesus did not view death as a dead end like we usually do, so he used the word "sleep." His use of this figure of speech reflected the observer's point of view. Jesus was not teaching a void of consciousness awaiting resurrection (Luke 23:43).

Paul wrote, **When the perishable puts on the imperishable, and the mortal puts on immortality, then shall come to pass the saying that is written: "Death is swallowed up in victory"** (1 Corinthians 15:54 ESV). Jesus was well aware of the criticism of him not preventing Lazarus' death. He heard them say it! (John 11:37). Therefore, he taught them that the gift of eternal life was the victory over death for those who believe. Jesus said to her, **I am the resurrection and the life. Whoever believes in me, though he die, yet shall he live, and everyone who lives and believes in me shall never die. Do you believe this?** (John 11:25-26 ESV). There is life beyond the grave.

The death of a believer must be accepted with a post-resurrection knowledge of Jesus Christ. **But in fact Christ has been raised from the dead, the firstfruits of those who have**

fallen asleep (1 Corinthians 15:20 ESV). Christ is the forerunner among those who will pass through death victoriously awaiting their resurrection.

Paul mentioned death without a "sting." Is that possible? Paul fully acknowledged the reality of death of the body but refused to believe in its finality. A person who is overcome by a problem is much less likely to find the solution. We have a choice to let the ugliness of death overwhelm us, or to believe in Jesus who has overcome death.

> **So is it with the resurrection of the dead. What is sown is perishable; what is raised is imperishable. It is sown in dishonor; it is raised in glory. It is sown in weakness; it is raised in power. It is sown a natural body; it is raised a spiritual body. If there is a natural body, there is also a spiritual body.** 1 Corinthians 15:42-44 ESV.

Paul wrote those words to encourage the Corinthians that there is hope in Christ as we go through the experience of the death of the body.

The new birth brings a fundamental change in the believer's relationship to death. The fear of death is broken by the promise of God that we will not be judged for our sins. No Christian is supposed to consider death of the body as a punishment. **There is therefore now no condemnation for those who are in Christ Jesus. For the law of the Spirit of life has set you free in Christ Jesus from the law of sin and death** (Romans 8:1-2 ESV). The law of sin is eternal judgment for unforgiven sins, but the Christian believer is forgiven. This is one place where the Christian can break the law with God's blessing!

When the fear of death is gone, we stop wasting the precious minutes of life by trying to fight off every wrinkle of age. We do not make vain attempts at self-deification like a Roman Emperor or attempt a modern day freezing of the brain to avoid returning to dust. Some cultures even buried their dead beneath the floors of their homes to keep loved ones continually close as long as possible, even if in a decaying state.

Christians believe the words of Jesus that he has gone before us through death to prepare a better future for us. Through trusting in God, we are at peace with the reality of Paul's statement about life:

> **So we are always of good courage. We know that while we are at home in the body we are away from the Lord, for we walk by faith, not by sight. Yes, we are of good courage, and we would rather be away from the body and at home with the Lord.** 2 Corinthians 5:6-8 ESV.

A Christian understands by faith in the scriptural revelation that death is not an ending of life but a move closer to God and the resurrection to come. A Christian finds comfort in God's promise of a future eradication of death from the entire universe and accepts God's timing and purpose in this matter. This is seeing the big picture of the Bible.

Our expectation of the resurrection of the body is our anticipation of participation of life with Jesus (1 Corinthians 15). Paul explained that death entered the world by Adam's sin and spread throughout mankind. Jesus demonstrated the victory of God over death itself by his own resurrection from the dead. Then he promised to share that victory with those who will follow him. What truly stoked the first disciples was the reality of the resurrection of Jesus.

The fact that Christ has already been raised is the basis of faith that God will fully reverse the effects of the curse when we join him in resurrection life. In the meantime, the gift of God is eternal life when we believe. The ability of death to destroy is nullified when our sins are forgiven because we cannot die guilty after receiving forgiveness. Our guilt was taken away at the cross of Christ. When we heard the gospel our response was to receive him personally by faith as Lord and Savior. On the merit of Jesus Christ alone, all future prosecution for our sins was cancelled.

In a key statement about the resurrection Paul wrote,

> **For as in Adam all die, so also in Christ shall all be made alive. But each in his own order: Christ the firstfruits, then at his coming those who belong to Christ. Then comes the end, when he delivers the kingdom to God the Father after destroying every rule and every authority and power. For he must reign until he has put all his enemies under his feet. The last enemy to be destroyed is death.**
> 1 Corinthians 15:22-26 ESV.

No wonder death is so hard to understand. Paul said it is the ultimate enemy. Perhaps God has determined that if His Son had to experience death with hope, despite the agonies, that it is not too much to require those saved for eternity to follow in his steps, glorifying God with their faith. Physical death has its sorrows but has lost its sting for those with faith in Jesus.

LEARNING TO MAKE GOOD CHOICES

At the beginning, Adam had the ability to know how to choose right from wrong, even before he knew good from evil. God warned him not to eat of the tree of knowledge of good and evil because when he ate from it, he would die.

God created us with the ability to choose between alternatives and holds each of us responsible to make the right choices. This is how He made us, and it was "very good" in his sight. The mercy of God is that from the foundation of the world He also provided a remedy for the evil He knew would come by our wrong choices.

Paul wrestled with these issues of making good and not bad choices in the book of Romans. To save time and mental stress, here is the summary version of Paul's book.

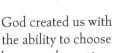

God created us with the ability to choose between alternatives and holds each of us responsible to make the right choices.

1. Yes, the whole of the creation was indeed very good at its creation and reflected well the inconceivable glory of the Being who made it all. **For the invisible things of him, from the creation of world, are clearly seen, being understood by the things that are made, even his eternal power and Godhead** (Romans 1:20 KJV). Any thinking person who opens their eyes knows that whoever created this wonderful life and universe is an entirely different order of Being than us.

2. **...sin came into the world through one man, and death through sin, and so death spread to all men because all sinned** (Romans 5:12 ESV). The problem of the world is sin, and the curse of God on sin is death.

3. We are created, and God is Creator, so **who are you, O man, to answer back to God? Will what is molded say to its molder, "Why have you made me like this?"** (Romans 9:20 ESV). Read the whole chapter in Romans 9 for some pride-humbling teaching. No more excuses allowed. The root of the problem is sin in us that chooses to serve self instead of God. **For all have sinned and fall short of the glory of God** (Romans 3:23 ESV).

4. As beautiful as the earth, universe, and life are in many ways, the creation is suffering from a malady that makes continuation of sinful life unsustainable. Any physicist will tell you that the universe is irreversibly dissipating into a

randomness of silent, lifeless atoms. As any honest sociologist will tell you, human beings always degenerate into selfishness and social strife.

In Romans 1 Paul told us the heavens declare the glory of God, but by chapter 8 he explained that on earth the world was caught in a bondage to corruption that is persistent, both physically and morally. **We know the whole creation groans and travails in pain together until now** (Romans 8:22 MKJV). Paul chose the word "travail," also used for childbirth, meaning that the pain has a forward-looking purpose of birthing a new life.

5. Nevertheless, God is working to guide the whole of his creation through the present evil into the promise of "perfection," which will infinitely surpass the starting point of "very good." We need to know God's plan in order not to despair. Like Paul, we take comfort in looking for the promise of a new heaven and earth. **The creation itself will be set free from its bondage to corruption and obtain the freedom of the glory of the children of God** (Romans 8:21 ESV).

In the big perspective, at the end of this era, God is going to ban "Death" itself from his new heaven and earth (Rev 21:4, 20:14). This is hard for our minds to grasp since it is a metaphysical concept. Death has become personified. We understand, however, how death was foreign to God's original plan when he created us.

Death appears inevitable now in creation, but for God it has always been unnatural and unwanted. **The Lord is not slow to do what he has promised, as some think. Instead, he is patient with you, because he does not want anyone to be destroyed, but wants all to turn away from their sins** (2 Peter 3:9 GNB).

6. Contradicting the despair, Paul wrote, **The creation itself also shall be delivered from the bondage of corruption into the glorious liberty of the children of God** (Romans

8:21 MKJV). The removal of death is one and the same as removing the curse made upon mankind for sin. This is what Jesus Christ has accomplished. God's solution for death is His plan to restore the physical creation and place it back on the path of God's original goal of life. Look at the last verse again: the creation will follow God's children into "glorious liberty." God is preparing us to reign and rule with Jesus Christ.

The Genesis revelation made clear that Adam's choice to sin did indeed bring death upon himself and on all of us. But God has poured out his Spirit of life upon us as a benefit of the resurrection of Jesus. **There is therefore now no condemnation for those who are in Christ Jesus. For the law of the Spirit of life has set you free in Christ Jesus from the law of sin and death** (Romans 8:1-2 ESV). The law of sin and death meant that sin brought death. The Spirit of life in Christ Jesus destroys death in us.

7. How does this work out for us personally? He will use you! God's plan will prevail in the churches through a process of forgiveness, cancellation of the curse individually, and guidance into personal maturity with the character of Jesus as the standard. **Having gifts that differ according to the grace given to us, let us use them** (Romans 12:6 ESV).

Jesus is returning as Lord of the nations and has ordained many helpers. He will resurrect his faithful saints first and appoint them to rule with him because they are living in eternal life. **Blessed and holy is he that hath part in the first resurrection: on such the second death hath no power, but they shall be priests of God and of Christ, and shall reign with him a thousand years** (Revelation 20:6 KJV).

WHAT ABOUT YOU?

For God so loved the world that He gave His one and only Son, that whoever believes in Him shall not perish but have eternal life. God did not send the Son into the world to condemn the world, but in order that the world might be saved through Him. John 3:16-17 TLV.

If you have not believed in Jesus yet, I urge you to put your faith in him. He is the Savior who reconciles us to God, as promised for two millennia before his birth in the Jewish Scriptures. He died as the sacrifice of a sinless life given in death for our sakes, to reconcile us to God.

The life and death of Jesus Christ is well attested in history. The Bible shows us the spiritual meaning of the facts, how that Jesus went to his death purposefully, providentially, and peacefully. Then He rose from the dead powerfully, promptly, and permanently. This is the historical account of the salvation God offers us.

There were eyewitnesses to Jesus who would not receive him as Messiah (Matthew 28:17). So, becoming a Christian is more than learning the facts about Jesus. The image of God was so clearly in him that a study of his life will reveal the character of God. People had the opportunity to take it or leave it. The problem for many was not his ministry, but the requirement to humble themselves and admit their sins. But to those who did believe in him, who saw in him the plan of God to reconcile the world to himself, he gave the right to become children of God. **He came to his own, and his own people did not receive him. But to all who did receive him, who believed in his name, he gave the right to become children of God** (John 1:11-12 ESV).

More than that, he rose on the third day proving that God is a God of life and forgiveness. He promises the same resurrection life to us. God is real and invites you to come to Him through faith in Jesus. Come into a living relationship with Him that will last for eternity. Ask God as your heavenly Father to forgive you because Jesus died for sinners. Receive Jesus into your heart as the risen Son of God and our Savior and learn to follow him daily through the inward guidance of the Holy Spirit of God.

Part 4

The Death of Death

He will swallow up death forever; and the Lord
GOD will wipe away tears from all faces, and
the reproach of his people he will take away
from all the earth, for the LORD has spoken.

Isaiah 25:8 ESV

THE END OF THE AGE

Death is the greatest enemy of mankind. The sad truth is

The defeat of death is the most important item on God's "To Do" list.

that Adam brought death on himself and then passed it on to all his descendants. The defeat of death is the most important item on God's "To Do" list. But as Paul wrote, **Each in his own order... The last enemy to be destroyed is death** (1 Corinthians 15:23-26). God has set the defeat of death at the very end of the age to highlight that it is the main problem in the world today.

The ultimate defeat of Death requires a great deal of finesse on God's part. As the saying goes, "Don't throw the baby out with the bathwater." He needed a better plan than to destroy the whole universe the day Adam sinned because it would have contradicted His original purpose of creating all persons for the enjoyment of life with Himself. Therefore, He loved his creation, and delayed the judgment. **But God shows his love for us in that while we were still sinners, Christ died for us.** (Romans 5:8 ESV).

God's plan of salvation was to separate humanity from the grip of death *before* the final judgment. Because God respects the free will of each person He has created, His plan of salvation has been the reconciliation of sinful persons as individuals to Himself from Adam down to the present day. This must be accomplished "One on one," as His Holy Spirit moves upon our spirits.

God sent His Son to be believed in through the gospel message. He will see that Jesus is preached to the ends of the earth before the end of the age. **And this gospel of the kingdom will be proclaimed throughout the whole world as a testimony to all nations, and then the end will come** (Matthew 24:14 ESV).

Throughout history God has watched over his creation with a purpose of life and not death. The devil rejoiced in death while God called for "repentance unto life" (Acts 11:18). From the first temptation of Eve to disobey God, the devil gained the power of death because humanity yielded to his temptations. God offered life. This spiritual battle revealed the moral character of God and the immoral character of Satan.

We do not have to wait until the end of this era to see the victory of God coming into the world. Jesus told the disciples; **I saw Satan fall like lightning from heaven. Behold, I have given you authority to tread on serpents and scorpions, and over all the power of the enemy, and nothing shall hurt you** (Luke 10:18-19 ESV).

In the second world war "D-Day" was the operation name for the return of the Allied armies to the continent of Europe at the beaches of Normandy. Within eleven months the war was over. Years ago, I traveled with my father over some of the roads the soldiers travelled from the Normandy coast inland to Germany. He was one of those soldiers who bled on those roads. The battles were very hard fought.

We visited the gravesides of thousands of Germans and Americans that died there. Some of them he had known. Jesus told us there are still spiritual battles ahead, but he has crossed the sea and breached the enemy's line ahead of us. He was the first raised from the dead so that he could accompany us all the way to the final victory over death. Many of us believe that there is not far to go to victory day.

SIGNPOSTS OF THE COMING END OF DEATH

One of the men in my father's infantry company designed and cast models of the historical milepost markers erected to commemorate the advancing liberation forces. Any war is progressive by fits and starts of many battles. On God's highway of history, He has given us road markers in His battle of the defeat of death. These signposts are in the ministry of Jesus.

1. **His physical healing miracles**. Jesus announced the impending invasion of the Kingdom of God into the earth with a campaign of physical healing. They were signs of his authority over creation, and evidence of God's kindness and intent to bring an end to suffering and death. **But the testimony that I have is greater than that of John. For the works that the Father has given me to accomplish, the very works that I am doing, bear witness about me that the Father has sent me** (John 5:36 ESV). The healings established him as a greater prophet and teacher than John the baptist. This was not to down-play John, but to punctuate the message of God that Messiah was now here.

2. **His resurrection miracles.** Jesus was not the first prophet to raise the dead. However, he did it more than once. When he raised Lazarus he made the astonishing claim, **I am the resurrection and the life. Whoever believes in me, though he die, yet shall he live, and everyone who lives and believes in me shall never die. Do you believe this?** (John 11:25-26 ESV).

Not only was the power of God at work through Jesus, but Jesus revealed that being the Messiah he was the unique Son of God and One with the Father. In the future, he will personally raise all dead bodies back to life; some to eternal life and some to judgment. As Messiah, the Savior, he calls us to put our faith in him for a resurrection defeat of death in our own lives. Martha's statement of faith is a model for us. She said to him, **Yes, Lord; I believe that you are the Christ, the Son of God, who is coming into the world** (John 11:27 ESV).

3. **His own Resurrection.** It is one thing to raise someone from the dead and another degree of difficulty to raise oneself. **For this reason the Father loves me, because I lay down my life that I may take it up again. No one takes it from me, but I lay it down of my own accord. I have authority to lay it down, and I have authority to take it up again. This charge I have received from my Father** (John 10:17-18 ESV). Jesus was the first person to be raised with a heavenly resurrection. He told John in a vision, **I died, and behold I am alive forevermore, and I have the keys of Death and Hades** (Revelation 1:18 ESV).

The bodily resurrection of Jesus proved that "going to heaven" is not a transition of our bodies from flesh to spirit. In other words, we do not become angels. Jesus's resurrection body was spiritually empowered. It was of a new order that we cannot understand, wherein Jesus owns the "keys of Death and Hades" because he rules over them. This is a glimpse of what is ahead for us who are united with him by faith.

In Jesus there was evidence of the progress of God's plan to defeat death. In divine healing, in the resurrection of Lazarus to a natural body, and in the resurrection of Jesus to a spiritually empowered new body, there was an evident salvation and a manifest deliverance. These are a foretaste of God's kingdom coming into the world we now occupy.

> In Jesus there was evidence of the progress of God's plan to defeat death.

THE LAST JUDGMENT

When we read the Scriptures, we find a large amount of revelation of the future. God wants us to know He has a plan to align the purpose of our lives with His purpose. Jesus taught us to pray about the future in the "Lord's prayer" when he instructed his disciples to pray, **Your kingdom come, your will be done, on earth as it is in heaven** (Matthew 6:10 ESV). This was not a mere hope in God's mind; it was a statement of His plan. Living with divine perspective is to live with hope and faith of the incoming kingdom from heaven.

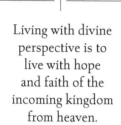

Living with divine perspective is to live with hope and faith of the incoming kingdom from heaven.

At the end of the current age, it is the plan of God to put Death itself to death. This was clearly a preaching emphasis of the apostle Paul. **Then comes the end, when he delivers the kingdom to God the Father after destroying every rule and every authority and power. For he must reign until he has put all his enemies under his feet. The last enemy to be destroyed is death** (1 Corinthians 15:24-26 ESV).

Although the condemnation of Adam's sin was pronounced the same day he sinned, God imposed death on the world as a process of two deaths, and both "deaths" were in the future. Physical death would take place at the end of each person's span of physical life. Secondly, a sentencing hearing of eternal punishment was set for the end of the current earth age. This will be a single event for all people who have ever lived. That event in Scripture is described as "the great white throne judgment" (Revelation 20:11). Commonly it is referred to as the final or last judgment.

Paul taught that before believing in Christ every person was "dead to God" because there was no personal relationship with God. This was a figurative use of the word "death," but the spiritual estrangement is very real. **And you were dead in the trespasses and sins in which you once walked** (Ephesians 2:1-2 ESV). One of the aspects of being under the condemnation of death was a broken communication with God. This was another use of the word "death" that is neither physical death nor the second death. When Jesus died physically bearing our

144

punishment of death, he restored the broken relationship with God through the death of his flesh (Hebrews 10:19,20).

But "death" is also the final condemnation for evil deeds that is earned like wages. A person's separation from God leads directly to physical death and thereafter to the second death for all persons not reconciling to God in the days of their life on earth. Jesus taught that the natural state of all persons was a life lived in a dead state towards God (Luke 9:60). That is why a "new birth" is necessary (John 3:3).

For the wages of sin is death, but the free gift of God is eternal life in Christ Jesus our Lord (Romans 6:21-23 ESV). The "second death" of eternal punishment is the opposite of God's gift of eternal life in Christ. It is worse than physical death because Jesus spoke of it as a conscious, continual experience of physical death. **And if your eye causes you to sin, tear it out. It is better for you to enter the kingdom of God with one eye than with two eyes to be thrown into hell, 'where their worm does not die and the fire is not quenched'** (Mark 9:47-48 ESV).

Jesus quoted the words of the prophet Isaiah about the fire and the worm. Isaiah in the last chapter of his prophecies was looking far into the future end of the age, when all kinds of death, and degrees of punishment, are tied together in the last days. The punishment of Adam's sin with death will then be understood as the all-consuming judgment it always was. There will be no more time for grace.

When the apostle John wrote about our relationship with God, he said that all people are *currently* under the condemnation of death, but by faith in Jesus's death and resurrection we can be removed from condemnation. **Whoever believes in him is not condemned, but whoever does not believe is condemned already, because he has not believed in the name of the only Son of God... Whoever believes in the Son has eternal life; whoever does not obey the Son shall not see life, but the wrath of God remains on him** (John 3:18 and 3:36 ESV).

Paul wrote the same truth to the church at Colossae. **And you, who were dead in your trespasses and the uncircumcision of your flesh, God made alive together with him, having forgiven us all our trespasses, by canceling the record of debt that stood against us with its legal demands. This he set aside, nailing it to the cross** (Colossians 2:13-14 ESV).

The death sentence conviction we carry with us naturally from Adam is real but can be cancelled through repentance and faith in Jesus as the Son of God. The last judgment will result in the "second death" that will be a sentencing impossible to reverse. Without receiving forgiveness of sins the inherited condemnation in Adam will follow through to a legal sentencing at the final judgment, along with condemnation for personal sins (Romans 5:12).

AN URGENT CALL TO REPENTANCE

The two deaths are related in this fashion. Repentance and reconciliation to God must occur before each individual's physical death. The judgment event at the end of the age will be based upon the books of God containing the recorded deeds of humanity (Revelation 20:12). The record of a person's life's works was completed at death and recorded in God's books. **And I saw the dead, small and great, stand before God; and the books were opened: and another book was opened, which is the book of life: and the dead were judged out of those things which were written in the books, according to their works** (Revelation 20:12 KJV).

If reconciliation with God is not made before death, it will be too late. There is no more time because our bodily life has ended, completing our deeds. This truth is plainly taught by Jesus. He called it "dying in your sins." At death an individual's choices are completed by which one either lives or dies eternally. **I told you that you would die in your sins, for unless you believe that I am he you will die in your sins** (John 8:24 ESV).

John the Baptist preached with urgency. He preached this way because repentance was still possible.

> **Even now the axe is laid to the root of the trees. Every tree therefore that does not bear good fruit is cut down and thrown into the fire. I baptize you with water for repentance, but he who is coming after me is mightier than I, whose sandals I am not worthy to carry. He will baptize you with the Holy Spirit and fire. His winnowing fork is in his hand, and he will clear his threshing floor and gather his wheat into the barn, but the chaff he will burn with unquenchable fire.** Matthew 3:10-12 ESV.

God in His mercy allows time for repentance while we are alive. Our earthly court system may require immediate punishment, or, allow for hearings that progress toward a final ending. First there is an arraignment hearing, then a conviction at the end of a trial, followed by a sentencing hearing for announcement of the severity of the penalty as determined by a judge. Lastly a court order is given for the surrender of the guilty person to authorities to begin the sentence. God also has a stepped plan in His death penalty process. In the human court system, there is a provision made for appeals or a delayed time before implementation of punishment so that there may be time for a commutation of sentence by a higher authority. So also, God has a process.

When God allows a person to live out their life, there is opportunity for every one of us to be humbled by our own sin. The pride of youth often mellows into teachability in maturity. Death cannot be blamed on Adam alone because we are all Adam doing deeds that we know are wrong. As the apostle Paul wrote, **for all have sinned and fall short of the glory of God** (Romans 3:23 ESV).

What about those who never had the opportunity to live to an age of accountability for their actions? Of course, the God who put all the stars in their courses in the universe has an answer for that question. But He is not under obligation to tell us how He works out those cases.

Abraham did not know all the answers, but he knew enough to stand by his faith in God's righteousness. **Far be it from you to do such a thing, to put the righteous to death with the wicked, so that the righteous fare as the wicked! Far be that from you! Shall not the Judge of all the earth do what is just?** (Genesis 18:25 ESV).

There are always questions. We must be patient to have the same faith as Abraham in God's righteousness when we do not know all the details. People like to throw out "what if" scenarios as a defense for their own guilt. Imagine a drowning person refusing a life preserver because he does not like the color of it! We should rather praise God for His plan to save. Ask God for an answer, and He will answer in His own time. He does not mind hard questions. Meanwhile, we can have a firm standing on what God has revealed.

Here is the wonder of the grace of God. If God had killed Adam on the day he sinned, humanity would have been destroyed and God's plan to share His life with us would be over. The devil would have won. The purpose of the devil is always to destroy what God values. But God had a plan to redeem us, giving us opportunity to repent during the days he has allotted each one of us before we die.

CREATED FOR GOOD WORKS

John boldly preached that true repentance will be evidenced in a changed life of good deeds. "Good works" is the result of real faith and was the constant refrain from all the apostles. For Paul, this is the purpose of "being saved" because Jesus **gave himself for us to redeem us from all lawlessness** and to purify for himself a people for his own possession who are zealous for good works** (Titus 2:14 ESV). This is personal accountability to the maximum degree.

God loves good works and so should we. A believer in Jesus does not trust that his good works provide forgiveness for his bad works at the judgment. Forgiveness is through the merit of the death of Jesus alone. Paul wrote,

> **For by grace you have been saved through faith. And this is not your own doing; it is the gift of God, not a result of works, so that no one may boast. For we are his workmanship, created in Christ Jesus for good works, which God prepared beforehand, that we should walk in them.** Ephesians 2:8-10 ESV.

At the great judgment there are two kinds of records, called "books." The first books contain the recorded deeds of our lives, and the second is the "book of life." The book of life records our faith in God because through our faith in Jesus we received forgiveness of past sins when we put our faith in him. No one is saved by deeds (books of deeds), but only by our faith (book of life). The two sets of books represent the division of faith and works in our lives.

Even while Paul taught that God's gift of forgiveness was not based upon good deeds, he still says the grace of God will produce good works when we receive it. At the last judgment the books of deeds will show that every believer's faith was real, as shown by the works they did. The apostle Paul taught that God will reward good works of believers at the last judgment (1 Corinthians 3:14).

One day the people asked Jesus, **"What must we do, to be doing the works of God?" Jesus answered them, "This is the work of God, that you believe in him whom he has sent"** (John 6:28-29 ESV). People try to earn their forgiveness by tithing, fasting, praying in public, or walking up the church steps on their knees. God only accepts faith. As Paul wrote, **For by grace you have been saved through faith. And this is not your own doing** (Ephesians 2:8 ESV). God keeps two sets of books to remind us that our faith is a different category than our works.

LIVING THE LIFE

Those who trust in Christ have the assurance of exemption from eternal condemnation. **And just as it is appointed for man to die once, and after that comes judgment, so Christ, having been offered once to bear the sins of many, will appear a second time, not to deal with sin but to save those who are eagerly waiting for him** (Hebrews 9:27-28 ESV). Jesus dealt with the issue of sin at the cross by providing forgiveness for those who receive him with faith and love as Lord and Savior.

Putting personal sins behind, every believer is called to look ahead. This was Paul's attitude. He said it was an attitude of maturity. We cannot change the past, but we can learn from it. Paul taught Christians to stand on the past, not to trip over it. Any person's past is like walking in mud. In mud you must walk carefully and deliberately. If you do so, you can stay cleaner and not falter and fall back into it. **But one thing I do: forgetting what lies behind and straining forward to what lies ahead, I press on toward the goal for the prize of the upward call of God in Christ Jesus** (Philippians 3:13-14 ESV).

Because Jesus has life within himself, he is the source of life to every person who is united to him.**For as the Father has life in himself, so he has granted the Son also to have life in himself** (John 5:26 ESV). We are united in Christ to the true source of life, and the life of this created universe is only its shadow.

I have always loved the words of encouragement given by an angel of God when he released the apostles from prison. They were "guilty" of preaching about Jesus and healing the sick. He said, **Go and stand in the temple and speak to the people all the words of this Life** (Acts 5:20 ESV).The entirety of faith in God, including forgiveness of sins through the cross of Jesus, and healing and deliverance in his name, may be summed up as **"all the words of this Life."**

There is no easy and quick fix for the death that the sin of Adam brought into the world, but there is a thorough and permanent one. To counter the damage of death, God has planned for the light of life in his believers to grow and fill the world. This is a process. **For at one time you were darkness, but now you are light in the Lord. Walk as children of light** (Ephesians 5:8 ESV). Enjoy the walk.

> There is no easy and quick fix for the death that the sin of Adam brought into the world, but there is a thorough and permanent one.

Jesus said we are lights on a hill. **In the same way, let your light shine before others, so that they may see your good works and give glory to your Father who is in heaven** (Matthew 5:16 ESV).

We have the gift of eternal life now and forever, but if Christians sit around doing nothing except talk about their faith in God's free gift, that they are saved by faith alone, and saved without works, then they are putting their candle under a basket.

Jesus said, Your light is your good works. We just read it! **In the same way, let your light shine before others, so that they may see your good works and give glory to your Father who is in heaven** (Matthew 5:16 ESV). Do something to God's glory! If the lights go out in my house, I go looking for a blown breaker or a short in the wiring. I don't start questioning the reality of electricity! A failure to produce good works should not cause us to lose our faith, but to repent of wrong practices. Your doctrine may not be wrong, but your works may be incomplete. Look for the problem in the connection of faith and practice.

Therefore, Peter also wrote,

> **For this very reason, make every effort to supplement your faith with virtue, and virtue with**

> knowledge, and knowledge with self-con-
> trol, and self-control with steadfastness, and
> steadfastness with godliness, and godliness
> with brotherly affection, and brotherly affec-
> tion with love. For if these qualities are yours
> and are increasing, they keep you from being
> ineffective or unfruitful in the knowledge of
> our Lord Jesus Christ. 2 Peter 1:5-8 ESV.

Peter said we need to supplement doctrine with godly eth-
ical actions. Notice that without a supplementation of godliness and fruit of the Spirit, the knowledge of Jesus will be
ineffective and unfruitful.

If your life isn't different as a Christian, you might have
learned to quote somebody's doctrine about salvation, but
Jesus has not yet become Lord of your life. You need to be
connected. As they say, the rubber needs to meet the road.

Some other people have grown cold and need to repent for
losing their first love for Jesus (Revelation 3:2, John 13:10). And
when I say "some," I mean most Christians, most of the time.

An important part of living your best Christian life is the
hope you carry with your faith. The expectation of resurrection
with Jesus is so different from the hopelessness we used to live
in. We look forward to the return of Jesus as he has promised.

> But each in his own order: Christ the firstfruits,
> then at his coming those who belong to Christ.
> Then comes the end, when he delivers the
> kingdom to God the Father after destroying
> every rule and every authority and power. For
> he must reign until he has put all his enemies
> under his feet. The last enemy to be destroyed
> is death. 1 Corinthians 15:23-26 ESV.

In the ages to come the image of the dust in us will fade, and the image of the immortal Christ Jesus will grow. The image of the glorious God will be reflected in our glorified bodies. What a future of wonder and glory we have ahead!

> In the ages to come the image of the dust in us will fade, and the image of the immortal Christ Jesus will grow.

The first man was from the earth, a man of dust; the second man is from heaven. As was the man of dust, so also are those who are of the dust, and as is the man of heaven, so also are those who are of heaven. Just as we have borne the image of the man of dust, we shall also bear the image of the man of heaven. 1 Corinthians 15:47-49 ESV.

Remember that the hope that Paul preached about was not an uncertain longing. **Let us hold fast the confession of our hope without wavering, for he who promised is faithful** (Hebrews 10:23 ESV). Biblical hope is the expectation of the divine appointment into God's presence with joy. God, who loved us while we were still sinners, has appointed us for the inheritance of grown children who take their place in the family line. **The Spirit himself bears witness with our spirit that we are children of God, and if children, then heirs—heirs of God and fellow heirs with Christ, provided we suffer with him in order that we may also be glorified with him** (Romans 8:16-17 ESV). This awareness fills our lives with meaning and purpose.

THE END OF DEATH

The end of death for us individually will mean peace with God for eternity. Paul wrote that Jesus **was delivered up for our trespasses and raised for our justification. Therefore,**

since we have been justified by faith, we have peace with God through our Lord Jesus Christ (Romans 4:25-5:1 ESV). Having peace with God we are freed to live in fellowship with God. Death is ending and being swallowed up in our new life.

Paul always emphasized the value of the good and moral life to be lived now in the flesh. The eternal life we have as a gift of God starts at conversion in this life and continues beyond death to blossom into a fruit of eternal life that is indescribable in physical terms.

Death and Life in the kingdom of God are a "zero sum game." More life will mean less death. Less death will mean more life. **When the perishable puts on the imperishable, and the mortal puts on immortality, then shall come to pass the saying that is written: "Death is swallowed up in victory"** (1 Corinthians 15:54 ESV). Victory feeds on the death of death. Less death will mean more life. That is why the apostle Paul used the figure of speech that "death is swallowed up in victory."

This saying will be true at the second coming of Christ, but even a casual reading of Romans 6 will show you that the possibility of victory swallowing death is true right now in our lives.

> **Do you not know that all of us who have been baptized into Christ Jesus were baptized into his death? We were buried therefore with him by baptism into death, in order that, just as Christ was raised from the dead by the glory of the Father, we too might walk in newness of life.** Romans 6:3-4 ESV.

Jesus died so that by faith we may be united with him who died for us. What died at the cross was not our future but our past, the condemned life we used to live. We can say "Goodbye" to the old life because who needs the condemnation? Quite the opposite, when Christ was raised from the dead, we legally rose with him to a "newness of life." We live in a relationship with Jesus as Lord of all, and we are the subjects of his kingdom. The victory is already working within us. The death of our old life is swallowed up with our new calling and hope.

While it lasts, this life in the flesh needs to be evaluated in the light of the eternal. **If in Christ we have hope in this life only, we are of all people most to be pitied. But in fact, Christ has been raised from the dead, the firstfruits of those who have fallen asleep** (1 Corinthians 15:19-20 ESV). Paul knew that a wonderful life awaited us after this world. How? Years after Jesus died on the cross, he spoke to Paul directly from heaven. **Last of all, as to one untimely born, he appeared also to me. For I am the least of the apostles, unworthy to be called an apostle, because I persecuted the church of God** (1 Corinthians 15:8-9 ESV). Paul always encouraged us to base our future hope on Jesus who was raised from the dead as a literal fact, not merely in an apparition or a feeling, or a memory.

When John received the vision that later was recorded as the book of Revelation, Jesus appeared in that vision with the words: **Fear not, I am the first and the last, and the living one. I died, and behold I am alive forevermore, and I have the keys of Death and Hades** (Revelation 1:17-18 ESV). The keys of Death and Hades signify the authority of Jesus over these realities. He stated, **I died and behold I am alive forevermore**, thereby declaring the end of death was assured by his own death and resurrection.

The reality of the end of death was impressed upon the apostles who saw Jesus alive after his resurrection. Paul listed many of the apostles as eyewitnesses of his resurrection, including himself (1 Corinthians 15:3-11). The life of Jesus also became the pattern for us when we were united by faith to him, and his Spirit continues to live within us to reveal that new life.

This knowledge of the risen Jesus is life changing because the end of death is made real to us.

In him also you were circumcised with a circumcision made without hands, by putting off

> the body of the flesh, by the circumcision of Christ, having been buried with him in baptism, in which you were also raised with him through faith in the powerful working of God, who raised him from the dead.
>
> Colossians 2:11-12 ESV.

> And this is the testimony, that God gave us eternal life, and this life is in his Son. Whoever has the Son has life; whoever does not have the Son of God does not have life. I write these things to you who believe in the name of the Son of God that you may know that you have eternal life. 1 John 5:11-13 ESV.

John's teaching was clear that eternal life begins with faith in Jesus Christ as the unique Son of God and Savior of the world. Eternal life is our current possession. John also taught that all life began in this world under the powerful hand of the pre-incarnate Christ.**All things were made through him, and without him was not any thing made that was made. In him was life, and the life was the light of men** (John 1:3-4 ESV).

It should come as no surprise to us that the Son through whom we were created at the first is also the One through whom eternal life was offered to us. Where light has come in, darkness is banished. **In him was life, and the life was the light of men. The light shines in the darkness, and the darkness has not overcome it** (John 1:4-5 ESV). Where God's life enters, death is ended.

BORN OF WATER AND THE SPIRIT

God's curse in Genesis 3:14-19 was a judgment of death because God had already told Adam (who told Eve) that eating of the tree of knowledge of good and evil would bring death.

God pronounced the judgment on Adam that physical bodies would return to dust. Obviously, this passed on to every generation of his descendants. The apostle Paul confirmed this when he taught, **For as in Adam all die, so also in Christ shall all be made alive** (1 Corinthians 15:22 ESV).

When Jesus was talking to Nicodemus about spiritual truths, Jesus told him that every person must be born *of water and spirit* (John 3). In the conversation it became apparent that Jesus was speaking of the waters of natural birth and the spiritual life that comes from reconciliation with God.

Jesus was teaching Nicodemus about how life is expressed within us by our body and our spirit. Jesus made the comparison between our natural birth and our spiritual re-birth when our sins are forgiven. Just as our physical birth is the beginning of our life in the world, the day of our re-birth in our spirit is the beginning of our personal relationship with God. Sometimes this is called our "new nature."

This new start for life happens by the moving of the Spirit of God upon us. Jesus said it was mysterious, like trying to understand where the wind comes from. Nevertheless, it is a true change of life experience caused by the Holy Spirit. **The wind blows where it wishes, and you hear its sound, but you do not know where it comes from or where it goes. So it is with everyone who is born of the Spirit** (John 3:8 ESV).

In the opening of his gospel book John wrote about conversion to Christ as a birth-type experience. **But to all who did receive him, who believed in his name, he gave the right to become children of God, who were born, not of blood nor of the will of the flesh nor of the will of man, but of God** (John 1:12-13 ESV).This re-birth is spiritual new life arising out of death because we are replacing the condemnation of our sins and offences with God's forgiveness and the gift of eternal life.

This re-birth occurs in our spirit. Back in Genesis the condemnation of death on Adam included the loss of a personal relationship with God. Adam and all his descendants became "dead in trespasses and sins." Christ gave us life by the gift of eternal life that comes from putting faith in him as the Savior from death. This new life is a spiritual work in us. If it were knowledge only, we would receive a diploma. Because it is a work in our spirit, it is a new life that has the capacity for relationship.

I read the book <u>A Man Called Peter</u> about a month before I became a Christian. The book was about the spiritual experiences of the late Peter Marshall, written by his wife, Catherine Marshall. As I remember, in the book she wrote about a time when Peter was driving but had to stop the car and get out to pray about something. The story strangely affected me because I remember being strongly impressed with the thought, "This man did not just believe something about Jesus. This man had a personal relationship with Jesus."

Paul wrote: **But God, being rich in mercy, because of the great love with which he loved us, even when we were dead in our trespasses, made us alive together with Christ—by grace you have been saved–** (Ephesians 2:4-5 ESV). Those who were cut off from God and under the death sentence have been given a new life in Christ.

In the following verses Paul wrote, **For by grace you have been saved through faith. And this is not your own doing; it is the gift of God, not a result of works, so that no one may boast** (Ephesians 2:8-9 ESV).Like John wrote, this is not a re-birth that comes by the will of man, but by the working of the Holy Spirit as a gift from God.

Jesus told Nicodemus, **Do not marvel that I said to you, 'You must be born again'** (John 3:7 ESV). Nicodemus should have had a deeper understanding of the ways of God than the average person because he was an elder in the community. The condemnation of God through death was real. The only escape was a work by the Holy Spirit. Jesus said, **That which is born of the flesh is flesh, and that which is born of the Spirit is spirit** (John 3:6 ESV).

A Scripture that Nicodemus should have known was a prophecy of Ezekiel. **And I will give them one heart, and a new spirit I will put within them. I will remove the heart of** stone from their flesh and give them a heart of flesh, that they may walk in my statutes and keep my rules and obey them** (Ezekiel 11:19-20 ESV).

Likewise, the prophet Jeremiah wrote, **For this is the covenant that I will make with the house of Israel after those days, declares the LORD: I will put my law within them, and I will write it on their hearts... For I will forgive their iniquity, and I will remember their sin no more** (Jeremiah 31:33-34 ESV).

Now, after several thousands of years, God has revealed much more about the punishment of death in this world and how it is leading toward final judgment and eternity. Jesus told Nicodemus, **You must be born again** (John 3:7).He said that we need to be born spiritually by the Holy Spirit in addition to being born naturally in the flesh. Unless we do, we will not be able to participate in the coming new world God has prepared for those who love Him.

The new birth, being born again, is a knowable mystery. Millions have experienced it. From our side we hear the gospel call to make peace with God. We turn away from our sins in repentance and place our faith in Jesus's substitutionary death for us on the cross, believing he was raised from the dead to guarantee the forgiveness of our sins before the judgment seat of God. Then, after confessing our faith in him as the Savior whom God sent, we use the new life he has given us to start a spiritual relationship with him.

GOD MAKES DEATH SERVE HIM

Adam was given life in a physical world where God expected his growth and maturity. Isn't this why we have our own children-- to give them the opportunity for life? We have children with the hope that they will do better at life than we have done. We do not deter for fear of the hardships that we know will come.

Overall, we believe in the goodness of life. When we compare life with death, it increases our motivation to listen to

God, to be reconciled with Him, and to participate in the end of death as He has planned. Truly, we are His children.

Adam and Eve received a death sentence for their sin that affected themselves, their children, and even the earth itself (Genesis 3:17). God had commissioned them to rule the world with righteousness and godly wisdom (Genesis 1:28). Instead, sin and death spread physically and spiritually everywhere.

Paul wrote that God allowed the curse of death as a judgment, but He maintained the expectation of purging sin from his children, so that they can bear fruitful works, filling heaven and earth with His glory. **For the creation was subjected to futility, not willingly, but because of him who subjected it, in hope that the creation itself will be set free from its bondage to corruption and obtain the freedom of the glory of the children of God** (Romans 8:20-21 ESV). The mercy of God planned an escape for humanity from its own evil. By justice He gave the sentence of death to Adam for his sin, but by love He knew the punishment could be used to make us look back to God for deliverance.

God even makes death serve Him. Death draws the attention of sinners. Death prompts questions about life after the death of the body. Death scares us into a search for meaning in our lives. The closeness of death challenges us to evaluate the worth of our life.

Sometimes we daydream about how we would live life differently if we had the opportunity because deep down there is a feeling that we have lived life poorly. Paul voiced the exasperation we have all felt when he wrote, **Wretched man that I am! Who will deliver me from this body of death?** (Romans 7:24 ESV). He immediately answered his own question in the next verse. **Thanks be to God through Jesus Christ our Lord!** (Romans 7:25 ESV).

Your Kingdom Come

The kingdom of God is coming and will reach full manifestation with the arrival of the new heavens and new earth. John wrote about it in the book of Revelation. But that will come to pass because God had a plan to bring the rebellion of the devil and of humanity to a great judgment. He will clear the books on all the past before moving on to the heaven of gold and glory.

Western culture focuses on the "stuff" in heaven, but God focuses on the "who" in heaven. Jesus warned us not to focus on material things. **Therefore do not be anxious, saying, 'What shall we eat?' or 'What shall we drink?' or 'What shall we wear?'**... But seek first the kingdom of God and his righteousness, and all these things will be added to you** (Matthew 6:31,33 ESV).

That is why the Lord's Prayer (in the same sermon) has the words, **Your kingdom come, your will be done, on earth as it is in heaven** (Matthew 6:10 ESV).

The defeat of death in the universe is progressive. The expansion of the Kingdom of God is now taking place as the gospel of Jesus is preached in the world. As Jesus taught, **And this gospel of the kingdom will be proclaimed throughout the whole world as a testimony to all nations, and then the end will come** (Matthew 24:14 ESV).

Here are some reasons why the kingdom comes incrementally.

Firstly, God wants personal faith to grow. He is delaying the day of judgment so that the maximum amount of people may have eternal life. **The Lord is not slow to fulfill his promise as some count slowness, but is patient toward you, not wishing that any should perish, but that all should reach repentance** (2 Peter 3:9 ESV).

Secondly, He is raising up his people in union with Christ to lead the cleansing of the universe. **For the creation was subjected to futility, not willingly, but because of him who**

161

subjected it, in hope that the creation itself will be set free from its bondage to corruption and obtain the freedom of the glory of the children of God (Romans 8:20-21 ESV). If God wanted to do everything himself, He could do so. But He wants us to work with Him, so that we live within His power and purpose (Revelation 20:4). Jesus said that the Kingdom comes progressively in the parables he taught (Matthew 6:10, 13:24). He also taught that his disciples will be stewards of his rule (Mark 13:34).

Thirdly, God has ordained that if we are recipients of grace, then we should share the sufferings of Christ (John 15:20, John 13:16, Colossians 1:24-25). Frankly, God put his own Son through a horrible death for us. It is not too much for Him to invite us to share in Jesus's sufferings of persecutions as a witness to the world that God is true and is merciful. His sufferings took away sins, and our sufferings are evidence of his love for others through us. The redeemed ones join Jesus in his fight against death as the kingdom of God progresses in authority over the sin-weary creation (Daniel 7:13,14. Revelation 20:4).

Of course, fears of death are present in everyone at some time or other. To help us, Jesus declared death by persecution is an escape, not a defeat. **Be not afraid of them that kill the body, and after that have no more that they can do** (Luke 12:4). What the enemy plans as a dead-end grave, God makes a doorway to eternal blessing, beginning the same day in Paradise with himself (Luke 23:43, Acts 7:55-59).

Likewise, Paul assures believers that, **We are confident, I say, and willing rather to be absent from the body, and to be present with the Lord** (2 Corinthians 5:8 KJV). As his own death at the hands of the executioner approached Paul was rejoicing and not cowering (2 Tim 4:6-8). The power of God over the grave is the center of the Good News.

THE KINGDOM MESSAGE

There is some tension in biblical interpretation between the individual's experience with God and the work of God in the world at large. Is religion supposed to be about our personal reconciliation with God by forgiveness of sins, or is it to be about the ascension of Jesus as the ultimate world ruler? Should we focus on personal perfection or seek to enforce kingdom behavior through political action?

Jesus taught a kingdom concept and instructed his disciples to do the same. **These twelve Jesus sent out, instructing them, "Go nowhere among the Gentiles and enter no town of the Samaritans, but go rather to the lost sheep of the house of Israel. And proclaim as you go, saying, 'The kingdom of heaven is at hand'** (Matthew 10:5-7 ESV).Although Jesus sent the disciples to preach the kingdom, he did not send them to preach it internationally until after his resurrection. At the first, he told them to preach the kingdom of God to the Jews only. The Jewish culture was already versed in the ways of God, having been recipients of the accumulated revelations of God from the forefathers and prophets for two millennia. The nation had the spiritual education to become early adopters of faith in God's Messiah.

As we know, there was not a man or woman who stood with Jesus at his trial. When Jesus was asked about his role as a king, he claimed a spiritual kingdom, and disavowed war (John 18:36). The last mockery of Jesus was that of his kingship when a sign was placed on his cross half in jest: "The King of the Jews" (Matthew 27:29-31).

When the national leaders rejected Jesus as King, they rejected their heritage as the people of God. In the church age, the kingdom of God will be found in the people of the local churches until the last days when Israel repents as a nation. As the nation of Israel had two millennia to wait for Messiah's first coming, the churches of Jesus have had two millennia to spread the gospel to all nations.

After the public rejection of Jesus as the King of the kingdom, the plan of God centered on the church of Jesus. Jesus had predicted this would happen. The concept of the church is non-political and spiritual. The church is not a substitute for the kingdom of God. The kingdom of God was present in the people themselves because Jesus taught, **Nor will they say, 'Look, here it is!' or 'There!' for behold, the kingdom of God is in the midst of you** (Luke 17:21 ESV).

The churches were not an organization but a society of believers adaptable to any nation or place world-wide. At first the disciples expected an immediate resurgence of the political kingdom message, but Jesus told them to focus on the work of the Holy Spirit instead of national Israel (Acts 1:6,7). The Holy Spirit's presence is the inspiration and source of power of the people of God (see Acts 4:8 and 5:3).

Within a few days of Jesus returning to heaven after the resurrection appearances, the Spirit of God fell on them, and their identity as an assembly of believers empowered by the Holy Spirit was thrust upon them from above (Acts 2:41-42, Matthew 3:11).

Gradually the first church in Israel adjusted their faith in Jesus after the resurrection, as they laid aside their expectation of an immediate political kingdom with Jesus at its head. After some time, they even admitted that Gentiles could be saved directly without becoming Jews (Acts 11:18).

In his evangelism Paul followed a pattern of preaching Jesus first in small synagogues where Jews gathered as minorities in foreign cities. If they rejected him, as they did in Pisidian Antioch, he said, **It was necessary that the word of God be spoken first to you. Since you thrust it aside and judge yourselves unworthy of eternal life, behold, we are turning to the Gentiles** (Acts 13:46 ESV). Paul preached Jesus to the non-Jews also, emphasizing the resurrection.

The early churches were mixed groups of believers of Jewish and pagan backgrounds, united by personal experiences of the Holy Spirit, believing the fulfillment of Messianic prophecies in Jesus, and not allying themselves with any political group or nationality (Acts 10:44-48). Paul taught the people to pray for whichever King or Governor ruled over them in order that Christians could pursue godly, peaceful, and honest lives without harassment (I Timothy 4: 1-4).

The Bible does reveal a political restoration of the nation of Israel in the future when Jesus will return and enforce his lordship over the nations personally (Daniel 7:27, Revelation 15:4). The Jewish people suffered the loss of their nation only a few decades after the resurrection. Christians were less influenced by their Jewish roots after Judaism lost its nationhood. The Jewish character of the gospel faded as most believers were converted from Gentile cultures.

The direct preaching of the gospel to the Nations did not make it any easier to be a disciple of Jesus. The former Jewish skepticism that demanded signs was replaced by the pagan penchants for self-indulgence and philosophy. **For Jews demand signs and Greeks seek wisdom, but we preach Christ crucified, a stumbling block to Jews and folly to Gentiles, but to those who are called, both Jews and Greeks, Christ the power of God and the wisdom of God** (1 Corinthians 1:22-24 ESV).

Since then, the Holy Spirit has been nurturing the churches in the ways of God with varying degrees of responsiveness to His leading. Most churches have institutionalized, some have ritualized. Yet others have trivialized while others have proselytized. Some people have hypothesized that the only true churches have gone underground and remain small. Despite the failures and disgraces of Christian churches institutionally, the Holy Spirit has always been keeping the gospel message on the move and individuals have been coming to faith in Jesus in all generations and in varied circumstances. This has fulfilled what

Jesus taught about the kingdom of heaven coming incrementally into the world through the church (Luke 13:20-21).

THE MILLENNIUM

Paul taught that the Jewish people would have a remnant restored to faith in God after the gospel is preached worldwide and the church age is completed. **Lest you be wise in your own sight, I do not want you to be unaware of this mystery, brothers: a partial hardening has come upon Israel, until the fullness of the Gentiles has come in. And in this way all Israel will be saved** (Romans 11:25-26 ESV). There are many people teaching about the wars of the last days and the restoration of national Israel. Since this book focuses on the end of death, I will just mention these events in passing.

When Jesus returns, he will rule the world from Jerusalem. This will be called the Millennium, meaning the 1000-year rule of the world by Jesus (Revelation 20:4). It will be a demonstration of how good life can be when humanity follows the Lordship of Jesus, and demonic activity is curtailed. This will be the last era of earth's history and will end with the final rebellion against the rule of God. Immediately following this rebellion will be the final judgment.

Many people do not understand that the resurrection of God's believers is a thousand years before the final raising of the dead. Jesus will come back to take direct rule of the world in preparation for the last judgment. This era is called the Millennium. **Then comes the end, when he delivers the kingdom to God the Father after destroying every rule and every authority and power. For he must reign until he has put all his enemies under his feet** (1 Corinthians 15:24-25 ESV). That reign is prophesied to last 1000 years.

John prophesied these events unfolding before his eyes in a vision of the future (Revelation 1:19). The righteous believers in Christ are resurrected to rule with him during the millennial reign. In Revelation 20 John highlights the resurrected martyrs of Jesus being honored with positions of authority during the 1000 years of the reign of Jesus. Those martyred are given honor and prominence for their sufferings. **Blessed and holy is the one who shares in the first resurrection! Over such the second death has no power, but they will be priests of God and of Christ, and they will reign with him for a thousand years** (Revelation 20:6 ESV).

These saints will be witnesses to the defeat of death after their own resurrections. Because they belong to Christ, they will be able to say with him who gives them life, **I died, and behold I am alive forevermore** (Revelation 1:18 ESV). Paul wrote that a common saying among early Christians was, **If we have died with him, we will also live with him** (2 Timothy 2:11 ESV).

We will move on to the end of the Millennium because Paul taught that the end of the Millennium will be the final judgment that will bring an end to death itself.

THE GREAT WHITE THRONE JUDGMENT

The great white throne judgment event is at the end of the Millennium. It is the immense and final judgment for all people who have ever lived. This is the grand settlement of God, the end time settling of all accounts according to God's justice. This will be the last mention of all the ugliness of wicked thoughts and deeds of human history as the books of the deeds of every person are opened and judgment given. The prophetic words are few, but in Revelation 20:12 they set the stage of this climaxing event.

> **And I saw the dead, great and small, standing before the throne, and books were opened. Then another book was opened, which is the book of life. And the dead were judged by**

what was written in the books, according to what they had done. Revelation 20:12 ESV.

Let's look at this event in detail. Firstly, in John's vision all people who have ever lived are gathered before this judgment throne of God. Jesus taught there will be a future resurrection of every person for good or bad (John 5:28,29). John, who recorded those words, also wrote the prophecy of the final judgment. Those believers who are already resurrected to reign with Christ will be joined by the dead of all the ages who are also given resurrection bodies. The last resurrection immediately precedes the great judgment so that the assembled company will be all the people of all times.

Those who died unreconciled to God will be raised directly to the judgment event at the end of the 1000 years. God resurrects every person from the dead no matter where they died, land or sea, or how they died. The resurrected ones who have reigned with Christ for the 1000 years will also be there. Therefore, the gathering at the great white throne includes the living and the dead of all the past ages.

Secondly, "The books were opened." These multiple books are extensive because they are the deeds of all people over all time. Obviously, this is only possible with God.

Thirdly, "And another book was opened." A single book is opened alongside the books containing the deeds of humanity and suggesting that they are referenced together. It appears that a name from the "books of deeds" is first cross referenced to the single "book of life." If the name is found in the single book, then that person is exempt from condemnation because their sins are already forgiven through faith in Jesus. In this context, "condemnation" is the sentencing to the eternal torment which is "the second death."

The single book contains the names of those of us who have believed in Jesus or who were believers in God before Jesus came. These are they of the "first resurrection" and are exempt from condemnation through faith in God's forgiveness

(Revelation 20:6, John 5:24). These are the only persons who are given admittance to live in the "new heavens and earth." The single book is also called "the Lamb's book of life" in Revelation 21:27.

> God in His mercy allows time for repentance while we are alive.

Fourthly, John adds in Revelation 20:15 "and whosoever was *not* found written in the book of life was cast into the lake of fire." John mentions no instance where the books of the deeds of a person gave evidence for exclusion of an individual from the lake of fire. The unlawful deeds of each person is a witness to God's righteous judgment of sin.

Only those listed in God's book of life will escape condemnation. **Whoever believes in him is not condemned, but whoever does not believe is condemned already, because he has not believed in the name of the only Son of God** (John 3:18 ESV).

As I wrote before in the section entitled "The Second Death," there is no forgiveness granted for sins based upon some good deed done in life, but only if we have repented and believed in Jesus as the unique Son of God. Sin brings death. A drop of poison contaminates the whole cup. The final and complete forgiveness for sin is found in Jesus who died to pay the death penalty for our sins.

God is not stingy with His forgiveness, but He is thorough in judgment. No one escapes. Because Jesus never sinned, he was not worthy of death. He was free from condemnation so that he could give his life to pay the debt sinners owed. **Christ is the sacrifice that takes away our sins and the sins of all the world's people** (1 John 2:2 CEV). **You know that he appeared in order to take away sins, and in him there is no sin** (1 John 3:5 ESV). Jesus died as Savior in his first coming

> God is not stingy with His forgiveness, but He is thorough in judgment.

in the flesh. At the great white throne judgment, he will be revealed in his second coming as the righteous judge of all the earth (Matthew 25:31).

Immediately before the revealing of the great white throne, God will bring righteous justice to Satan (Revelation 20:7-10). His final defeat is the end of all his evil plans. He will be cast directly into the "lake of fire" for never-ending torment with all the demons who had rebelled with him. John saw the unfolding of future divine justice as if it had already happened in his vision.

THE FEAR OF CONDEMNATION IS ENDED

Blessed and holy is the one who shares in the first resurrection! Over such the second death has no power, but they will be priests of God and of Christ, and they will reign with him for a thousand years (Revelation 20:6 ESV).

The elimination of the fear of condemnation is a powerful inspiration and comfort to every believer. This is a consequence of the defeat of death by Jesus. There is complete deliverance from the fear of dying in our sins when our faith rests in Jesus as the Son of God.

The apostle John saw the risen Christ in a vision of his power and wrote about it at the beginning of the book of Revelation. **When I saw him, I fell at his feet as though dead. But he laid his right hand on me, saying, "Fear not, I am the first and the last, and the living one. I died, and behold I am alive forevermore, and I have the keys of Death and Hades"** (Revelation 1:17-18 ESV).

Jesus is glorious in the power of God precisely because he personally defeated death. He stands victorious after his death proclaiming, **Behold, I am alive,** as an encouragement to those who believe in Him. He holds the keys of Death and Hades so that he may unlock the chains that bind humanity and the universe. (Hades is the spiritual abode of the dead persons who await the final judgment.) He will resolve all the loose ends and deliver the kingdom to the Father as planned (1 Corinthians 15:24).

Adam was given responsibility for this physical world when God said to him, "Have dominion ... on the earth" (Genesis 1:28). After he disobeyed God, the condemnation of physical death was given to him, but it was another 930 years until his life on earth was over. The guilt of sin was immediate for Adam, but the sentence was incrementally enforced. Adam did not physically return to dust when God uttered the words of judgment. He lived 930 years more. God was allowing time for repentance by pronouncing a judgment that was real but delayed. This is similar to our modern legal system.

The condemnation was upon Adam and all his descendants. Each of us has received the same sentence because while we are alive we all approach ever closer to this personal, physical death. We are born with numbered days but live life as though we will never die and give account of our days to God. This is very strange behavior when you think about it. We don't like to speak of death, except when the subject is forced upon us.

There is a deep consciousness of the condemnation to death in all of us. Paul wrote in the book of Hebrews that the fear of death lies within all of us, and that salvation in Jesus will **deliver all those who through fear of death were subject to lifelong slavery** (Hebrews 2:15 ESV). I felt it when my father asked me to accompany him to a doctor's appointment where he feared a deadly prognosis.

Human death was first recorded when Abel was slain by his brother Cain, perhaps a few decades after Adam's sin. Paul says death came because of Adam: **Therefore, just as sin came into the world through one man, and death through sin, and so death spread to all men because all sinned** (Romans 5:12 ESV). Although Adam did not die the day he sinned, the judgment of death was spoken to him on that day, and death became universal and undefeatable as humanity's greatest enemy. People may dispute the existence of God, but no one denies that our bodies die.

The delay in death's arrival for each one of us allows God's Spirit to box us into a corner like a naughty child and speak directly to our hearts. "Your days are numbered; now is the best time to repent of your sins." The Psalmist prayed,

> **You have set our iniquities before you, our secret sins in the light of your presence. For all our days pass away under your wrath; we bring our years to an end like a sigh. The years of our life are seventy, or even by reason of strength eighty; yet their span is but toil and trouble; they are soon gone, and we fly away. Who considers the power of your anger, and your wrath according to the fear of you? So teach us to number our days that we may get a heart of wisdom** Psalms 90:8-12 ESV.

The delay in judgment also allows God to use the ugliness of physical death to teach us about the greater death in eternity. This is not a physical death, but an eternal punishment called "the second death" in Scripture. Jesus clearly warned about it. In one section of the gospel message of Mark, Jesus repeated this phrase: "Gehenna fire." Gehenna was the dumping ground of Jerusalem where the fire seemed to never stop.

Jesus was comparing an awful place on earth with the worse reality of a never-ending punishment (Mark 9:42-50). God put a delay between the offenses of sin and the final punishment, mercifully allowing us time and opportunity for repentance toward God and faith in Jesus.

I had just passed my twelfth birthday when I stared death in the face. My brother and I occupied the third floor of a large single-family home. On a cold night in March a shorted wire in the bedroom ceiling light slowly heated the ceiling area for several hours until it burst into flame in the attic. I awoke to my mother's screams as she stood in her nightgown illuminated by flames of fire breaking through the ceiling. We fled for our lives.

The firemen said it was only the thickness of the old plaster ceiling that kept us from being asphyxiated before my mother arrived. It had to be God who awakened her in the middle of the night in her bedroom a story below us, and caused her to come up the winding stairway, and traverse the width of the house through a long hallway, and through the door of our bedroom.

We ran down several flights of stairs, and I threw on a coat as we passed the first story closet and exited to the street. My bare feet felt strange in rubber snow boots. As the flames rose through the roof, I looked up from the street through the window of the dormer where my bed was located and saw the ceiling collapse in the fire.

I knew God was in that deliverance and for several years I prayed an anniversary prayer of thanksgiving. I still did not know how to find God through Jesus, but I was sensitized to the fragility of life and the closeness of death. On and off, I kept looking for spiritual truth. We all have opportunity though one or more of life's troubles to understand our need of God's salvation. God used a close contact with death to remind me I was dust animated by his gift of life.

There is grace available through Jesus Christ before we die physically. Like a request for a summary judgment to stop the prosecution, we can exit the judicial process of death by faith in Jesus. I am not a lawyer so perhaps my parallels to our justice system could be improved. God appears to have a legal pathway laid out for our acquittal, if we will make a plea deal based on Christ Jesus. Eternal punishment is inevitable if the prosecution proceeds to its conclusion. But if a plea bargain can be made on other grounds, the prosecution will not proceed, and we will be saved.

The gift of eternal life is applied to us the moment we believe. That is why Jesus said, **Truly, truly, I say to you,** whoever hears my word and believes him who sent me has eternal life. He does not come into judgment, but has passed from death to life (John 5:24 ESV).That life is eternal. This is peace with God. Receiving the gift of life means we have an exemption from condemnation at the great white throne judgment. Eternal punishment is the lake of fire originally prepared for the devil, and not for God's children (Matthew 25:41 ESV).

Physical death was pronounced on Adam in Genesis 3:19, but the second death of eternal hell will not come until the judgment is completed at the great white throne of Revelation 20. This permanent form of death is called "the second death" in Scripture. It is also called the "judgment." It is the last step of the "condemnation" (John 5:24).

The sentencing hearing for eternal punishment is at the great white throne judgment at the end of the history of the present earth. Although physical death reigned in all persons after Adam, this was only the first phase of death. The time for the judgment event that initiates eternal hell has been determined by God to occur after the Millennium. Jesus said that the believer "does not come into judgment" at this event. His words calm our fears.

There is an interesting question of timing here. John wrote that those who do not believe in Jesus *remain* condemned, but those who believe *will not* be condemned. Of course, before believers became believers they were under condemnation. At one point in their lives all persons were condemned, but then some who believe in Jesus are given a reprieve. This is why believing the gospel is "good news."

The effect of that reprieve is that believers in Jesus will not have to suffer the pronouncement of the second death in the future. In the book of Revelation John wrote, **Blessed and holy is the one who shares in the first resurrection! Over such the second death has no power** (Revelation 20:6 ESV).

Being "saved" in Scripture means not only being forgiven of past sins, but also means exemption from the current condemnation determined for the entire world. In the Scriptures, our salvation is both a current event and a future one. The condemnation will end in a sentencing of eternal punishment at the last great judgment of God on all unrepentant persons.

Paul wrote that salvation was completed and yet also is in process. This is because we are redeemed by the death of Christ at a point in time, and what is done cannot be undone. We appropriate the forgiveness of God through faith in Jesus. **Therefore, if anyone is in Christ, he is a new creation. The old has passed away; behold, the new has come** (2 Corinthians 5:17 ESV). At the same time, God has a plan of salvation for the universe that is in progress of unfolding. God respects our choices as individuals and is giving us opportunity now before the return of Jesus for repentance from our sins and faith in Jesus as the Son of God.

We are not static but growing. **He died for all, that those who live might no longer live for themselves but for him who for their sake died and was raised** (2 Corinthians 5:15 ESV). And later in the same letter Paul wrote, **being ready to punish every disobedience, when your obedience is complete** (2 Corinthians 10:6 ESV).

What if, when someone truly believed in Jesus, their skin would turn purple, or their face might continually glow! That might be a sign of the new birth easily visible to all who see it. But God has purposed that a maturity of Christlikeness is His goal, so He is not so concerned with marking the spiritual event of new birth, as much as He wants our lives to promote His glory by maturing in good deeds. **In the same way, let your light shine before others, so that they may see your good works and give glory to your Father who is in heaven**(Matthew 5:16 ESV).

Jesus died for our sins because physical death was the penalty imposed upon mankind when Adam sinned. By dying a death he did not deserve, Jesus bore our guilt of sin. In his submission to death on the cross, Jesus fulfilled the typology of all the animal sacrifices before him, wherein the innocent died for the sins of the guilty.

Jesus in his sufferings on the cross fulfilled the payment of this death penalty, legally removing from us any further prosecution for past offences. Our fear of condemnation will diminish as the changes in our character become apparent to us and others that God is working in us-- even if our skin does not turn purple.

His perfections made Jesus qualified to suffer death in the place of others. Peter said the sinlessness of Jesus was crucial to our forgiveness. **Knowing that you were ransomed from the futile ways inherited from your forefathers, not with perishable things such as silver or gold, but with the precious blood of Christ, like that of a lamb without blemish or spot** (1 Peter 1:18-19 ESV).

As the apostle John wrote, **He is the propitiation for our sins, and not for ours only but also for the sins of the whole world** (1 John 2:2 ESV). "Propitiation" is a technical word that is variously translated as "offering," "sacrifice," "payment," or "atonement." God made his salvation inclusive for the whole world, rather than exclusive. The gospel is an open invitation. You are not excluded. John wrote, **But to all who did receive him, who believed in his name, he gave the right to become children of God, who were born, not of blood nor of the will of the flesh nor of the will of man, but of God** (John 1:12-13 ESV).

But if we walk in the light, as he is in the light, we have fellowship with one another, and the blood of Jesus his Son cleanses us from all sin (1 John 1:7 ESV). The words "the blood of Jesus Christ" is not a symbol. It is a part that stands for the whole, a synecdoche. At the first Passover, the Hebrews did not nail a lamb's head on the doorpost to signify a death had occurred, but only applied the lamb's blood. The blood represented the whole of the lamb's life because God taught Moses that **it is the blood that makes atonement by the life** (Leviticus 17:11). The blood showed that the lamb was slain.

Jesus died because he shed all his blood for us when he laid down his life as the death penalty that our sins earned. In his last words on earth, Jesus said, **It is finished** (John 19:30). John wrote this because Jesus knew that **all things were now accomplished** (John 19:28). Jesus fulfilled his life's work and paid the price God required for the forgiveness of our sins when he died. Our fear of condemnation is ended today because Christ died for our sins: in history, in Jerusalem, as the ancient Scriptures had foretold.

STAYING FREE FROM SIN

The church of Jesus Christ at Corinth was at the center of Paul's heart. The grace of God was evident from the first when God told Paul in a dream before the church was started, **for I am with you, and no one will attack you to harm you, for I have many in this city who are my people** (Acts 18:10 ESV).

Was the church perfect, and did they live sinlessly after being saved? No, but they were "God's people." Paul's two long letters to the church in Corinth revealed their strengths and weaknesses. These two letters became two books of the New Testament because they addressed the issues every local church faces.

Paul had two main points he wanted them to understand. Firstly, the forgiveness of their sins was accompanied by God's gift of a new life that changed them forever. **Therefore, if anyone is in Christ, he is a new creation. The old has passed away; behold, the new has come. All this is from God, who through Christ reconciled us to himself** (2 Corinthians 5:17-18 ESV).

Secondly, they must hold to God's truth by living holy lives. **Strive for peace with everyone, and for the holiness without which no one will see the Lord** (Hebrews 12:14 ESV). It should not be a shock to Christians today that whoever believes in Jesus receives forgiveness for past sins and enablement to live a life pleasing to God.

The apostles followed what Jesus taught about the new life in Christ. **Truly, truly, I say to you, whoever hears my word and believes him who sent me has eternal life. He does not come into judgment, but has passed from death to life** (John 5:24 ESV). There is no stronger assurance of salvation than we have in these words.

Of course, Jesus also expected us to live holy lives and not to use his free gift of forgiveness as an excuse to live indulgently. Jesus said, **Whoever has my commandments and keeps them, he it is who loves me. And he who loves me will be loved by my Father, and I will love him and manifest myself to him** (John 14:21 ESV).

Being "saved" means becoming a follower of Jesus Christ, and not just an admirer. Today we "follow" a famous person by reading about them in their social media posts. But Jesus taught that to follow him was to take up a cross, as he bore a cross. **Then Jesus told his disciples, "If anyone would come after me, let him deny himself and take up his cross and follow me. For whoever would save his life will lose it, but whoever loses his life for my sake will find it"** (Matthew 16:24-25 ESV).

Jesus made it clear that we are saved only once, yet it is still true that it is necessary to continually avail ourselves of his cleansing work in our lives. Jesus taught, **The one who has bathed does not need to wash, except for his feet, but is completely clean** (John 13:10 ESV). This teaching deserves some sincere consideration.

We can be completely clean and have the need for a foot washing at the same time. John was there when Jesus said those words, so this is the context for us to understand I John 1:9. **If we say we have no sin, we deceive ourselves, and the truth is not in us. If we confess our sins, he is faithful and just to forgive us our sins and to cleanse us from all unrighteousness** (1 John 1:8-9 ESV). The same grace that covered our past sins is available to us to cover our shortcomings as disciples.

OUR FOUNDATION IS THE RIGHTEOUSNESS OF CHRIST

There are two kinds of fear of God: the fear of eternal punishment, and the fear of displeasing God. When a Christian has been invited into God's family as a child of God, then the fear of God should end and be replaced with the fear of displeasing Him. When a person is initially "born again," then a new life begins.

Assurance of being a child of God is foundational to our being, therefore Jesus said we have "**passed from death to life**" (John 5:24). The issue of eternal salvation is completed -- at least so far as the new birth is concerned. Paul called this beginning of faith the "foundation" of Jesus Christ. **For no one can lay a foundation other than that which is laid, which is Jesus Christ** (1 Corinthians 3:11 ESV).

Being "born of God" (John 1:12-13) eliminates our fear of eternal punishment because Jesus has paid the debt of our sin with his own life. In the same transaction, the righteousness of Jesus is credited to us. **For if, because of one man's trespass, death reigned through that one man, much more will those who receive the abundance of grace and the free gift of righteousness reign in life through the one man Jesus Christ** (Romans 5:17 ESV).

What happens after we receive the gift of eternal life? In other words, what is the purpose of the Christian life? Paul taught that our works as children of God will be judged as good or bad. The context of this judgment is that God's children must learn to be zealous of good works. Jesus "**gave himself for us to redeem us from all lawlessness and to purify for himself a people for his own possession who are zealous for good works** (Titus 2:14 ESV).

The whole purpose of Jesus dying for us is to perfect us in righteous living. Why would he be satisfied with less? The Church is his bride. He told the church in Laodicea, **Those**

whom I love, I reprove and discipline, so be zealous and repent (Revelation 3:19 ESV). There will be times when Jesus loves us so much that he will make us shake in our boots. But we remain the love of his life.

Paul mentioned that this was the common experience of those believers in his churches.

> **Therefore, my beloved, as you have always obeyed, so now, not only as in my presence but much more in my absence, work out your own salvation with fear and trembling, for it is God who works in you, both to will and to work for his good pleasure.** Philippians 2:12-13 ESV.

Also, in Romans 11 Paul wrote, **They were broken off because of their unbelief, but you stand fast through faith. So do not become proud, but fear. For if God did not spare the natural branches, neither will he spare you** (Romans 11:20-21 ESV).

Paul was crystal clear in distinguishing between the fear of eternal judgment and the fear of our imperfections (sins) as believers. **For godly grief produces a repentance that leads to salvation without regret, whereas worldly grief produces death** (2 Corinthians 7:10 ESV). The context here was the Corinthian church cleaning up sinful behaviors in the church.

Paul warned the church that Christians would face a judgment of the value of their life lived for Christ. He was urging them to do their best, and in so doing he said they were building with "gold, silver, precious stones..." The primary reference of this passage in 1 Corinthians 3 is Paul's description of the efforts of missionaries called to start churches, but the principle applies to every Christian life.

As I explained in the last section, *The Fear of Condemnation is Ended*, confession of sin is needed whenever we sin. **If we confess our sins, he is faithful and just to forgive us our sins and to cleanse us from all unrighteousness** (1 John 1:9 ESV).

The apostle John was speaking of believers who had been saved a long time. Nobody lives a sinless life, even after being saved. Therefore, John wrote, **If we say we have not sinned, we make him a liar, and his word is not in us** (1 John 1:10 ESV). But confessed sin is covered and cleansed by the once for all sacrifice of Jesus on the cross.

If we properly understand the account of Jesus washing Peter's feet, we can maintain our assurance of salvation although we are not yet perfected. Jesus was preparing Peter for his biggest fall, the denial of knowing Jesus the next morning. He was teaching Peter that he is active in every step of our purification process of growing in Christlikeness, if we let him get close to us. When we read the whole account in John 13, we see that Jesus used Peter's situation as an object lesson that applies to all of us.

CONTINUALLY IMPROVING

Nevertheless, Paul was explicit about our responsibilities in this life. Notice that Paul connects our righteous behavior now in this life with "the day of Christ" which is the return of Jesus.

> **Do all things without grumbling or disputing, that you may be blameless and innocent, children of God without blemish in the midst of a crooked and twisted generation, among whom you shine as lights in the world, holding fast to the word of life, so that in the day of Christ I may be proud that I did not run in vain or labor in vain.** Philippians 2:14-16 ESV.

Paul said we are subject to an inspection, just as any building is subject to civil inspection to confirm the quality of construction. Paul compared the deeds of Christians to a construction project. **You are God's field, God's building. According**

to the grace of God given to me, like a skilled master builder
I laid a foundation, and someone else is building upon it.
Let each one take care how he builds upon it (1 Corinthians
3:9-10 ESV).

The future judgment of believers' works will scrutinize how
we lived our lives as children of God. Hopefully, God will have
reason to reward us, although some have not done much with
their lives other than to repent and believe in Jesus. Christians
are to exhort one another not to be complacent: But exhort
one another every day, as long as it is called "today," that
none of you may be hardened by the deceitfulness of sin
(Hebrews 3:13 ESV). On the positive side, Paul's teaching here
is not to bring the fear of condemnation back to those who are
trusting in Jesus for forgiveness, but to hold out the possibility
of rewards for righteous living.

We will all carry with us into the coming Kingdom of God a
portfolio of Christian works, a resume of what we have done
with our lives since we have been saved. When we are born
again, there is a break with the past. Paul was insistent that
there be no returning to the sins of the past.

> Or do you not know that the unrighteous will
> not inherit the kingdom of God? Do not be
> deceived: neither the sexually immoral, nor
> idolaters, nor adulterers, nor men who prac-
> tice homosexuality, nor thieves, nor the greedy,
> nor drunkards, nor revilers, nor swindlers will
> inherit the kingdom of God. And such were
> some of you. But you were washed, you were
> sanctified, you were justified in the name of
> the Lord Jesus Christ and by the Spirit of our
> God. 1 Corinthians 6:9-11 ESV.

Peter was also in disgust of those who gave up following Jesus
in righteous living.

> For if, after they have escaped the defilements of the world through the knowledge of our Lord and Savior Jesus Christ, they are again entangled in them and overcome, the last state has become worse for them than the first. For it would have been better for them never to have known the way of righteousness than after knowing it to turn back from the holy commandment delivered to them. What the true proverb says has happened to them: "The dog returns to its own vomit, and the sow, after washing herself, returns to wallow in the mire." 2 Peter 2:20-22 ESV.

This is very sobering to contemplate. It reminds us that God has restored us to be adults and to seek His help to mature in being Christ-like. We cannot remain as willful children but are to be mature and responsible.

Despite these warnings not to return to disobedience, Paul was upbeat about the grace of God. Jesus was the one who died for us "while we were sinners." That kind of love is not looking for an excuse to punish us; it is the love that has a plan to perfect us.

> Husbands, love your wives, even as Christ also loved the church, and gave himself for it; That he might sanctify and cleanse it with the washing of water by the word, That he might present it to himself a glorious church, not having spot, or wrinkle, or any such thing; but that it should be holy and without blemish. Ephesians 5:25-27 KJV.

The key idea for believers is to always be ready to receive correction as children of God. As Paul wrote, **Therefore, my beloved, as you have always obeyed, so now, not only as in** my presence but much more in my absence, work out your own salvation with fear and trembling, for it is God who works in you, both to will and to work for his good pleasure (Philippians 2:12-13 ESV).There is a delicate balance to be maintained within the confidence of our family relationship to God in Christ.

For those with open hearts to God, the blood of Jesus Christ is our confidence that our debt to God is paid in full. The apostle John wrote, **If we confess our sins, he is faithful and just to forgive us our sins and to cleanse us from all unrighteousness** (1 John 1:9 ESV). The context of this promise is that we cannot afford to dismiss our current sins as "nothing." John taught us in this passage not to lie about them but to confess them to God. Having done so, our confidence as a child of God is restored.

As King David once prayed after repenting of a serious sin, **Cast me not away from your presence, and take not your Holy Spirit from me. Restore to me the joy of your salvation, and uphold me with a willing spirit** (Psalms 51:11-12 ESV). A good parent hugs their child after a time of correction and confirms them in love. This is what God does to us.

God uses our remorse as a tool for change. As I wrote before in the section named *The Physical Death of Jesus on the Cross*, "As we mature, confession of our faults and weaknesses as sins turns into a prayer for righteous behavior in our body and spirit." My dad always told me to keep an honest score card when playing golf. Or else, he said, you will never know when you improve. That applies here, too.

Before the new heavens and earth arrive, God will clean up all unrighteousness in his creation. And that experience will not be all bad news because Paul said that there will be rewards given for the righteous works of believers. **If the work that anyone has built on the foundation survives, he will receive a reward** (1 Corinthians 3:14 ESV).

THE ARENA OF CHRIST'S VICTORY

I like to say that the death of Jesus by his shed blood is exactly what God said was the requirement to pay the penalty for our sins. We need to agree with God. Because in the Old Testament God said, "the life of the flesh is in the blood" (Leviticus 17:11), we know that physical death is the meaning of "shed blood" in the Bible. This is not superficial bleeding from a small cut in the flesh but a mortal wounding causing a "bleeding out" to death.

Death's days are numbered. In earth's history physical death has reigned like a brutal dictator in the world (Romans 5:14). The death of the body has taught the world the awfulness of the results of sin. Physical death should be a warning of the worse eternal punishment to come. God has used a delay before final punishment to allow time for repentance while each person lives out their physical life. God is still delaying enforcement of eternal punishment on sinners until all of us have lived out our lives. This life we live is an arena of critical decisions.

There is no mention of eternal death in Genesis 3, but eternal punishment is a part of the curse of death because humankind was made originally as a unity of flesh and spirit. Separation from God through sin affected our whole being. The spiritual and eternal effects of God's punishment of death were not explicit in Genesis 3 as death of the body was, but they became clearer with later revelation from God.

Although Genesis 3 does not mention eternity, the immediate punishment given to Adam was the curse of death from which followed the loss of fellowship with God and a denial of access to eternal life. After the pronouncement of death to Adam and Eve, they were banned from the garden of God, and access to the tree of life was forbidden.

When God addressed the sin of the first couple, the curse of death was set into motion, and it was like tipping over the first piece in a long line of standing dominoes. **Therefore, just as sin came into the world through one man, and death through sin, and so death spread to all men because all sinned—** (Romans 5:12 ESV).

Further revelation of eternal life and eternal punishment would come later after Adam's sin. In this world now, death rules. Today we know that God has set a future date for a "sentencing hearing" after the Millennium of Christ for the second death. All these consequences combined are the punishment of death that Adam received when he sinned.

The curse of death should be understood as an extended process of death that God predicted would happen if Adam sinned. **But of the tree of the knowledge of good and evil you shall not eat, for in the day that you eat of it you shall surely die** (Genesis 2:17 ESV). The Hebrew is more literally translated as "in the day that you eat of it, dying you will die." The near-Easterner repeated a word twice for emphasis. After Adam's sin, death spread to all persons. God was warning that if death came, it would be truly bad news.

In practice, all people experience life as a process in which death is unavoidable. We mature to adult age in twenty years, but then "aging" comes as a process built into us that reveals death at work, progressing a little bit every day until the body is dead.

Physical death became real the day God pronounced it (Genesis 3:19). Although eternal punishment will not begin until the end of the Millennium when the great white throne judgment is concluded, physical death filled the world after Adam's sin, and is currently the cutting edge of God's judgment.

Physical death came into the world as a punishment but also as a lesson to fear the "second death" that lasts without end. Jesus taught, **But I will warn you whom to fear: fear him who, after he has killed, has authority to cast into hell. Yes, I tell you, fear him!** (Luke 12:5 ESV).

The delay in final judgment allows a period of time for repentance. The reality of physical death does not exclude eternal punishment but emphasizes that the arena of conflict is now between God and Satan *in this physical world*.

Jesus came in a body of flesh and blood *into this physical world* because that is the arena where humanity is currently under the sentencing of physical death. God allowed life to continue after the entrance of sin into His creation because salvation is still possible while people are in the flesh for a physical lifetime.

There is a spiritual warfare aspect to death that Paul mentioned: **Since therefore the children share in flesh and blood, he himself likewise partook of the same things, that through death he might destroy the one who has the power of death, that is, the devil** (Hebrews 2:14 ESV). Jesus entered our life of flesh and blood to defeat a condemnation of death abiding on the guilty. He offered his death in the place of ours as an innocent substitutionary sacrifice. In theology this is called "the atonement."

Since the condemnation of death came to Adam in this physical world, Jesus came into our world to pay the penalty of sin with his own life. No matter what "power of death" the devil had, Jesus by his cross and resurrection has demonstrated his Lordship over life and death (Revelation 1:18).

In the Old Testament kingdom of Israel God described the physical death of an innocent sacrificial animal as a payment that covers our sin when the sacrifice was offered in faithful obedience to God's instruction. God was connecting the physical and spiritual dimensions by accepting the physical life of an animal as a covering for our broken spiritual relationship to God. We need to always keep in mind that the arena of Christ's victory over death in this physical world solved the problem of death in both the physical and spiritual dimensions.

Beyond the seriousness of physical death, God has continued to warn humanity of the far worse eternal death that lay ahead. Jesus warned us, **And do not fear those who kill the body but cannot kill the soul. Rather fear him who can destroy both soul and body in hell** (Matthew 10:28 ESV).

Sinners are under the condemnation of physical death now in this life *and* a second death in the world to come. The present condemnation on every unrepentant person is progressing toward the physical judgment of death but is not concluded until the great white throne judgment with "the second death." Eternal punishment is inevitable for sinners who do not repent but is avoidable for those who do repent.

The arena of this conflict, however, is not in eternity, but has always been in this physical world. This world is where Adam ate from the forbidden tree, where God pronounced that the reward of sin is our body returning to dust, and where God defended the placement of his image on physical Adam and Eve by prescribing capital punishment for the sin of murder (Genesis 9:6). This is why Jesus, the eternal Word of God, took on flesh and died for the sins of others *in this physical world*.

At the last judgment, the witness of the books of the deeds of men and women will be the basis of eternal condemnation. It is by the shedding of his blood in this world at the cross that Jesus secured our redemption by bringing forgiveness of sins. It is within his own person that the physical and spiritual dimensions of life are united, and the debt of sin is paid in full in his body by death.

> **He entered once for all into the holy places, not by means of the blood of goats and calves but by means of his own blood, thus securing an eternal redemption ... how much more will the blood of Christ, who through the eternal Spirit offered himself without blemish to God, purify our conscience from dead works to serve the living God.** Hebrews 9:12-14 ESV.

A perfect physical life offered to God was of inestimable value when offered by the leading of the Holy Spirit. The blood of Christ was not inferior in the sight of God because it was physical. Sadly, some commentators have denied this truth.

The spirituality of Jesus was not holier than his flesh. The sinlessness of his life in the flesh qualified him as the sacrifice for sin who brought to us every spiritual blessing. **Blessed be the God and Father of our Lord Jesus Christ, who has blessed us in Christ with every spiritual blessing in the heavenly places** (Ephesians 1:3 ESV).

New Testament soteriology does not require us to reject physical offerings and exalt spiritual ones. That is a pagan Greek conception of the divine, not that of the God of the Bible. The words of Jesus and his apostles in the Scriptures represent his physical life as the high cost paid for our sin, and his sinlessness was the quality of that life. Jesus offered his physical life's blood through the Spirit of God for a perfect offering that redeems us eternally. **Knowing that you were ransomed from the futile ways inherited from your forefathers, not with perishable things such as silver or gold, but with the precious blood of Christ, like that of a lamb without blemish or spot** (1 Peter 1:18-19 ESV).

In God's view, human life is not a defilement of the world, but human sin is what defiles us (Matthew 15:18).

> **The earth is the LORD's and the fullness thereof, the world and those who dwell therein, for he has founded it upon the seas and established it upon the rivers. Who shall ascend the hill of the LORD? And who shall stand in his holy place? He who has clean hands and a pure heart, who does not lift up his soul to what is false and does not swear deceitfully. He will receive blessing from the LORD and righteousness from the God of his salvation. Such is the generation of those who seek him, who seek the face of the God of Jacob.** Psalms 24:1-6 ESV.

Physical death was the sentence that was pronounced upon Adam in Genesis. Physical death on the cross was the focus of Jesus. There are many that have not understood this truth. They think the cross must not only be a payment of physical death, but that they must find in it also a payment-in-kind by a spiritual death of Jesus that corresponds to a sinner's estrangement from God.

—————+—————

Separation from God is a result of our sin, not the punishment for it.

Such commentators do not understand that separation from God is a result of our sin, not the punishment for it. The punishment for our sins was death, so Jesus died for our sins. But this brings us into a depth of theology that requires its own book.

FINAL THOUGHTS

In closing this book, let's summarize some key points. The physical death of Jesus was sufficient to redeem us. God imposed a sentence of physical death on Adam in Genesis 3, so that "in Adam all die" (1 Corinthians 15:21-22). Death is the decreed punishment for sinners.

—————+—————

Death is the decreed punishment for sinners.

Behold, all souls are mine; the soul of the father as well as the soul of the son is mine: the soul who sins shall die (Ezekiel 18:4 ESV). Sinners who die "in their sins" (unforgiven) will also face eternal torment called "the second death" (John 5:19-47).

Those who believe in Jesus as Messiah, the Savior, will be saved from that "second death," and have received forgiveness of sins because Jesus bore the punishment of death in their place when he shed his life's blood to death on the cross (Leviticus 17:11). The forgiveness of sins, the new birth in our spirit, and eternal life are all gifts of God that we received when we believed in Jesus as Son of God (John 5:24).

Speaking of the price of our redemption, Jesus said, **I am the living bread which came down from heaven: if any man eat of this bread, he shall live for ever: and the bread that I will give is my flesh, which I will give for the life of the world** (John 6:51 KJV). Jesus felt no compulsion to cloak the forgiveness of sins he offered in "spiritual" language, although he did use analogies and figures of speech.

He said plainly, "the bread is my flesh." He said, "I lay down my life." He said, **I am the good shepherd. The good shepherd lays down his life for the sheep** (John 10:11 ESV). He said, **Destroy this temple, and in three days I will raise it up.** When John wrote this quote in his gospel, he added a comment: **But he was speaking about the temple of his body** (John 2:19-21 ESV).

The arena of our sin is this world. Appropriately, Jesus took on our human nature in a natural body without sinning, in order to fight the battle for our deliverance in this world. He died a real death by crucifixion on the cross for the forgiveness of all who would believe in him.

THE DEATH OF DEATH

By the wisdom of God, He will truly bring an end to Death itself. This goes far beyond simply removing His children in Christ from the presence and experience of death. That alone is wonderful. But when God conducts the final judgment on sin, the condemnation will be to remove Death itself from His presence and Kingdom. **Then Death and Hades were thrown into the lake of fire. This is the second death, the lake of fire.** (Revelation 20:14 ESV). If you can wrap your mind around it, Death will die eternally in God's lake of fire, which is called the second death.

The new heavens and new earth will be God's restoration of the creation, purged of all the punishments of the past. I think it will be the completion of what God intended for the first earth had sin not entered. **He will wipe away every tear from their eyes, and death shall be no more, neither shall there be mourning, nor crying, nor pain anymore, for the former things have passed away** (Revelation 21:4 ESV). In this eternal kingdom of God, the word "death" will not be spoken because it will have no meaning. Everything will be life because we will live directly by the gift of life from God Himself.

In this eternal kingdom of God, the word "death" will not be spoken because it will have no meaning.

The curse of the judgment of death will be no more because the plan of God for its eradication will be completed.

> **No longer will there be anything accursed, but the throne of God and of the Lamb will be in it, and his servants will worship him. They will see his face, and his name will be on their foreheads. And night will be no more. They will need no light of lamp or sun, for the Lord God will be their light, and they will reign forever and ever** Revelation 22:3-5 ESV.

Amen and Amen!

About the Author

Richard writes for every reader who wants to learn about Jesus from the Bible. He is a parent of six grown children and has nine grandchildren. He has lived life as a Christian working for a computer manufacturer, as an instructor in computer science, and as a real estate professional. He has pastored in churches for over two decades. He has a B.A. in Economics and a Master of Divinity degree in Bible study and pastoral care. His internet blog site is www.BlogOnGod.org.

Printed in the USA
CPSIA information can be obtained
at www.ICGtesting.com
LVHW011509230424
778177LV00009B/24